Evagrius of Pontus

Talking Back

CISTERCIAN STUDIES SERIES NUMBER TWO HUNDRED TWENTY-NINE

Evagrius of Pontus

Talking Back
A Monastic Handbook for Combating Demons

Translated with an Introduction by
David Brakke

α

Cistercian Publications
www.cistercianpublications.org

LITURGICAL PRESS
Collegeville, Minnesota
www.litpress.org

A Cistercian Publications title published by Liturgical Press

Cistercian Publications
Editorial Offices
Abbey of Gethsemani
3642 Monks Road
Trappist, Kentucky 40051
www.cistercianpublications.org

Evagrius of Pontus, Saint, c. 345–399

Talking Back translated from the edition of
Wilhelm Frankenberg
Euagrios Ponticus

Abhandlungen der königlichen Gesellschaft der
Wissenschaften zu Göttingen,
Philologisch-historische Klasse, Neue Folge 13.2
Berlin: Weidmannsche Buchhandlung, 1912

New Testament quotations are from *New Revised Standard Version Bible*, copyright © 1989 National Council of the Churches of Christ in the United States of America. Used by permission. All rights reserved.

1   2   3   4   5   6   7   8   9

Library of Congress Cataloging-in-Publication Data

Evagrius, Ponticus, 345?–399.
    [Antirrhetikos. English]
    Talking back : a monastic handbook for combating demons / Evagrius of Pontus ; translated with an Introduction by David Brakke.
        p. cm. — (Cistercian studies series ; no. 229)
    In English, translated from a Syriac translation of the Greek original.
    Includes bibliographical references (p.) and indexes.
    ISBN 978-0-87907-329-9 (pbk.)
        1. Spiritual warfare. I. Brakke, David. II. Title. III. Series.

BV4509.5.E82513 2009
248.8'942—dc22

                                                                2009004768

To Mary Jo Weaver

experienced in the movements of the soul and the ways of prayer

Contents

Acknowledgments

I completed a rough translation of *Talking Back* while I was an Alexander von Humboldt Fellow at the Institut für Ägyptologie und Koptologie of the Westfälische Wilhelms-Universität Münster. I am grateful to the Humboldt-Stiftung for its generosity and to my host, Stephen Emmel, for his hospitality and support. William Harmless encouraged me to undertake this project and responded to an early portion of my translation. Robert Sinkewicz offered sage advice and generously shared with me his own working translation of *Talking Back*. Kevin Jaques lent me his expertise in Arabic as I studied Loukios's letter to Evagrius. Rowan Greer read a draft of the entire book and made several important suggestions and corrections, and Mary Jo Weaver did the same for the Introduction. A group of students in Syriac at Indiana University read portions of the text with me. I have presented the ideas found in the Introduction to several audiences, who responded with helpful questions and comments, especially at the North American Patristics Society, the History of the Book Seminar at Indiana University, and the Fifteenth International Conference on Patristic Studies (2007) at the University of Oxford. E. Rozanne Elder of Cistercian Publications greeted my project with enthusiasm and patience, and the anonymous readers provided welcome endorsements of my efforts. Father Mark Scott of Cistercian Publications and Colleen Stiller of Liturgical Press and her staff produced this book with intelligence and care. As always, Bert Harrill has provided me with endless moral support. I am grateful to all of these persons and institutions; the shortcomings of this work are my own.

Portions of the Introduction repeat material from my *Demons and the Making of the Monk: Spiritual Combat in Early Christianity* (Cambridge, MA: Harvard University Press, 2006).

Introduction

Sometime in the final decade of the fourth century, a monk named Loukios wrote to Evagrius of Pontus, one of the leading spiritual guides among the monks of the Egyptian desert. Calling him "honored father," Loukios asked Evagrius to compose for him a treatise that would explain the tactics of the demons that try to undermine the monastic life; Loukios hoped that such a work would help him and others to resist more successfully the evil suggestions that the demons made. In response, Evagrius sent Loukios a letter, now known as his fourth, and a copy of the work translated here: *Antirrhētikos*, or *Talking Back*. Among the monks of late antiquity and early Byzantium, it became one of the most popular of Evagrius's books: ancient authors regularly mentioned it in their discussions of Evagrius, and it was eventually translated from the original Greek into Latin, Syriac, Armenian, Georgian, and even Sogdian.

Talking Back has not enjoyed the same level of popularity among modern students of early Christian monasticism. One reason for this neglect is linguistic: both the Greek original and the Latin translation are lost; complete texts survive only in Armenian and Syriac manuscripts that are either not fully edited or difficult to access. But also *Talking Back* concerns itself exclusively with the monk's combat with demons, a topic that has not interested many modern historians and theologians, most of whom have directed their attention to social and cultural features of early monasticism or to aspects of monastic spirituality that appear more directly relevant to contemporary persons, such as prayer or spiritual direction. Intense conflict with demons, however, especially in the form of thoughts, lay at the heart of the early Egyptian monk's struggle for virtue, purity of heart, and thus for salvation.[1] Opposition from demons, whether they tempted the monk to sin or tried to frighten him into abandoning the ascetic life, provided the resistance that the monk needed to form himself into a person of integrity. In *Talking Back* we find the thoughts, circumstances, and anxieties with which the demons assailed the monk, and we observe a primary strategy in the struggle to overcome such assaults: *antirrhēsis*, the speaking of relevant passages from the Bible that would contradict or, as Evagrius puts it, cut off the demonic suggestions.

Evagrius of Pontus crafted the most sophisticated demonology to emerge from early Christian monasticism and perhaps from ancient Christianity as a whole.[2] Born around 345 to a country bishop in the region of Pontus in Asia Minor, Evagrius showed religious and intellectual promise even as a teenager and was ordained a reader by Bishop Basil of Caesarea. He then became the protégé of Gregory of Nazianzus, serving as Gregory's archdeacon when he became bishop of Constantinople in the late 370s and assisting him in his efforts in behalf of Nicene theology. It is traditional to believe that Evagrius received his grounding in an Origenist Christian theology under Gregory and subsequently

---

[1] See David Brakke, *Demons and the Making of the Monk: Spiritual Combat in Early Christianity* (Cambridge, MA: Harvard University Press, 2006), and Antoine Guillaumont and Claire Guillaumont, "Démon: III. Dans la plus ancienne littérature monastique," *Dictionnaire de spiritualité ascétique et mystique: Doctrine et histoire* (1957) 3:189–212.

[2] On Evagrius's demonology see Brakke, *Demons and the Making of the Monk*, 48–77, and Guillaumont and Guillaumont, "Démon: III. Dans la plus ancienne littérature monastique," 196–205. For more extensive introductions to Evagrius's life and thought, see Evagrius of Pontus, *The Greek Ascetic Corpus*, Oxford Early Christian Studies, Robert E. Sinkewicz, ed. and trans. (Oxford: Oxford University Press, 2003); A. M. Casiday, *Evagrius Ponticus*, The Early Church Fathers (London and New York: Routledge, 2006); and William Harmless, sj, *Desert Christians: An Introduction to the Literature of Early Monasticism* (New York: Oxford University Press, 2004), 311–71.

learned about ascetic practice and demonic conflict from monks in Egypt, but we shall see below that there is evidence that even Gregory may have contributed to his knowledge of the demons and of strategies against them. In any event, Evagrius's discipleship under Gregory came to an end when Gregory had to resign his episcopal seat and Evagrius fled to Jerusalem after he fell in love with a married woman.

In Jerusalem Evagrius suffered an emotional and physical breakdown, and the ascetic leader Melania the Elder persuaded him to take up the monastic life in Egypt. In the deserts of Nitria and Kellia, Evagrius apprenticed himself to monks such as Ammonius and the two Macarii—Macarius the Great (or the Egyptian) and Macarius the Alexandrian—from whom he must have received much of his advanced knowledge about demons and combat with them. Evagrius soon emerged as an authoritative teacher in his own right, and around him gathered a group of monks that at least one contemporary author called "the circle around Evagrius." Supporting himself as a calligrapher, Evagrius counseled the monks who visited him and with whom he gathered weekly for worship and fellowship, and he produced a large number of literary works of great variety, not only practical treatises on the monastic life, but also works of biblical exegesis and of advanced theology. Even these latter works, however, support Evagrius's vision of monasticism in which bodily discipline, demonic conflict, prayer and psalmody, biblical study, and speculation on higher theological questions all played important roles in forming the monk into a "gnostic," a knower of God. *Talking Back* may be focused on the very practical problem of resisting demonic suggestions, but the scope and precision of both its attention to the monk's soul and its treatment of the Bible reveal the creativity and intelligence of a great theologian.

Literary Form and Function: A Manual for Spiritual Combat

After a prologue, *Talking Back* collects 498 biblical passages, each preceded by the person, thought, or situation to which it should be addressed during demonic conflict. The passages and their usually brief directive introductions are arranged in eight books according to the eight primary demons that Evagrius claimed attack the monk: gluttony, fornication, love of money, sadness, anger, listlessness, vainglory, and pride. Because of numbering errors in the manuscript that has served as the primary basis for modern study of the work (B.L. Add. 14,578), modern scholars have not always recognized that there are 498 entries, and in fact the scribe of the manuscript mistakenly counted 497.[3] I discuss this issue more fully in the Note on Texts and Translations. There are also numbering problems in Book 3 at 3.19–27, which I have noted there and taken into account in my translation.

The work is identified by a variety of titles in antiquity, but the most likely title is *Antirrhētikos*, which I have translated, following Elizabeth Clark, *Talking Back*.[4] The scribe of the best-known manuscript simply called it, "A Treatise of Evagrius on the Eight Thoughts," but ancient authors give it more specific titles. Evagrius himself in his letter to Loukios calls it "the treatise of responses" (*Ep.* 4.1), although it is not clear that he means this to be a formal title. Around 420, the bishop and former monk Palladius states in his *Lausiac History* that Evagrius "composed three sacred books, so-called responsories (*antirrhētika*), for monks, proposing strategies against the demons."[5] Palladius's reference to three books may be puzzling, but there can be no doubt that our work is what he means. The *Life of Evagrius* preserved in Coptic, whose original author was most likely Palladius, provides another certain reference to our work:

> If you [sing.] want to know the experiences that he [Evagrius] underwent at the hands of the demons, read the book he wrote against the responses of the demons [*oube niouohem ntenidemōn*].

---

[3] Among the few scholars who have seen that there are 498 entries is, as one might expect, Gabriel Bunge; see his "Evagrios Pontikos: Der Prolog des 'Antirretikos,'" *Studia Monastica* 39 (1997): 77–105, at 78.

[4] As far as I can tell, Clark was the first person to translate the title into English as *Talking Back* in her *Reading Renunciation: Asceticism and Scripture in Early Christianity* (Princeton: Princeton University Press, 1999), 131.

[5] Palladius, *Lausiac History* 38.10. See the Bibliography for full bibliographical data for ancient works referred to in the footnotes.

You will see their full power and various temptations. Indeed, it was for these reasons that he wrote about these subjects, in order that those who read about them might be comforted knowing that they are not alone in suffering such temptations, and he showed us how such thoughts could be mastered through this or that kind of practice.[6]

The phrase "against the responses of the demons," with its attribution of "responses" to the demons rather than to the monk, may be a garbled translation of a Greek title that included the terms "against" and "responses," perhaps "Responses against the Demons." It is likely that the Coptic *Life of Evagrius* attests either a book on Egyptian monasticism that Palladius wrote before the *Lausiac History* or an earlier version of the *History* itself.[7]

Writing in the decades after Palladius, the church historian Socrates Scholasticus provides a list of Evagrius's works, including "the *Antirrhētikos* from the holy Scriptures against the tempting demons, divided into eight parts according to the number of the eight thoughts."[8] Socrates lists the *Antirrhētikos* third, after the *Praktikos* and the *Gnostikos*, an order that perhaps Palladius had in mind when he referred to "three sacred books" in the *Lausiac History*. Here the Greek title, in its use of an adjective ending with *-ikos* to describe the subject of the book, parallels the other two books of Evagrius, lending support to its being the accurate title.

Toward the end of the fifth century, in his continuation of Jerome's *Illustrious Men*, Gennadius of Marseilles began his list of the books of Evagrius by stating:

---

[6] Coptic *Life of Evagrius* 21; trans. Tim Vivian, *Four Desert Fathers: Pambo, Evagrius, Macarius of Egypt & Macarius of Alexandria: Coptic Texts Relating to the "Lausiac History" of Palladius*, Popular Patristics Series (Crestwood, NY: St. Vladimir's Seminary Press, 2004), 85, altered. The Coptic text is edited by E. Amélineau, *De Historia Lausiaca, quaenam sit huius ad monachorum aegyptorum historiam scribendam utilitas* (Paris: Leroux, 1887), 115–16.

[7] Gabriel Bunge and Adalbert de Vogüé, *Quatre ermites égyptiens: d'après les fragments coptes de l' 'Histoire Lausiaque,'* Spiritualité Orientale 60 (Bégrolles-en-Mauges: Bellefontaine, 1994); Vivian, *Four Desert Fathers*, 46–52.

[8] Socrates, *Ecclesiastical History* 23.37.

> Against the suggestions of the eight principal vices, which he
> was the first to observe or among the first to teach, he com-
> posed eight books with testimonies from the holy Scriptures.
> Doubtless he was imitating the Lord, who always met his
> attacker with testimonies from the Scriptures, so that a sug-
> gestion of whatever kind, whether from the devil or from
> vicious nature, might have a testimony against it. By request
> I translated this work into Latin with the same simplicity that
> I found in the Greek.[9]

As disappointing as it is for the modern scholar to read about a
fifth-century Latin translation of *Talking Back* that apparently does
not survive, this brief notice is instructive in other ways. Gennadius
speaks not, as Evagrius does, of the eight principal demons or
thoughts, but of the eight principal *vices*, and he states that suggestions to vice may come either from Satan or from humanity's
fallen nature. When Gennadius says that Jesus "always" responded
to his attacker with scriptural testimonies, he seems to refer not
only to Jesus' temptation from the devil, the model that Evagrius
cites in his prologue, but also to Jesus' entire career, including his
interactions with human as well as demonic opponents (e.g., Mark
2:23-27). Gennadius's use of the term *vices* reflects the inward turn
in how Evagrius's teachings were appropriated in the West. John
Cassian had initiated this trajectory by speaking more frequently
of vices than of demons and by situating the monk's conflict with
temptation more within the interior division between the fallen
human being's spirit and flesh than within Evagrius's cosmic division between human beings and demons.[10] Gennadius, then, says
that the evil suggestions that require refutation come not only
from the demons but also from our own vicious nature.

Gennadius considered *Talking Back* an example of "testimonies
from the Scriptures" (*testimonia Scripturarum*), an important clue to
how ancient readers, or at least Latin-speaking Christians, might
have understood the genre of the work.[11] Ancient people created

---

[9] Gennadius of Marseilles, *Illustrious Men* 11; *Patrologia Latina* 58:1066-67.

[10] Brakke, *Demons and the Making of the Monk*, 242–46.

[11] Unlike other scholars, I am not convinced that the seventh-century Syrian
Christian Dadisho of Bet Qatraye gives our work the title *Demonstrations from*

anthologies of excerpts from written works for a variety of purposes, including private study, research for one's own work, and self-improvement. Christians created anthologies of excerpts from the Bible or "testimonies" primarily for apologetic reasons, to defend Christological and ecclesiological claims, and for moral exhortation, to encourage virtue and discourage vice.[12] Scholars debate whether already in the first or second century Christians had created "testimony books" of excerpts from the Septuagint in order to support their teachings about Christ and the inclusion of the Gentiles; such books, if they existed, may have served a polemical function in debates with nonbelieving Jews. Certainly by Evagrius's time, however, such works existed. Transmitted among the Latin works attributed to Cyprian of Carthage (d. 258) are *To Fortunatus* (or *Exhortation to Martyrdom*), which collects scriptural excerpts in support of martyrdom, and *To Quirinus* (or *Testimonies Against the Jews*), in which such excerpts serve to condemn the Jews, promote Christological claims, and exhort to proper moral behavior.[13] Closer to Evagrius's own context are fragments from a Greek papyrus codex, dated to the fourth century, in which messianic verses from Isaiah, Genesis, 2 Chronicles, and

---

the *Holy Scriptures* when he cites *Ant.* 7.37 (see, e.g., René Draguet's translation in Corpus scriptorum christianorum orientalium 327:140, and Adam H. Becker, *Fear of God and the Beginning of Wisdom: The School of Nisibis and the Development of Scholastic Culture in Late Antique Mesopotamia*, Divinations: Rereading Late Ancient Religion [Philadelphia: University of Pennsylvania Press, 2006], 190). I translate: "Those [books of Aristotle] are the ones that the blessed Evagrius condemns with the demonstrations from the holy Scriptures that he sets out in the book against the eight passions of sin and against the inciting demons. For among those that he sets out against the demon of vainglory he says the following . . ." (*Commentary on the Book of Abba Isaiah* 13.4; Corpus scriptorum christianorum orientalium 326:181).

[12] In general, see Martin C. Albl, *"And Scripture Cannot Be Broken": The Form and Function of the Early Christian "Testimonia" Collections*, Supplements to Novum Testamentum 96 (Leiden: Brill, 1999).

[13] Cyprian, *Ad Quirinum, Ad Fortunatum*, ed. R. Weber, Corpus Christianorum Series Latina 3/1 (CCSL 3/1) (Turnhout: Brepols, 1972); Cyprian, Treatise 11 [To Fortunatus] and Treatise 12 [to Quirinus], Alexander Roberts and James Donovan, eds., The Ante-Nicene Fathers vol. 5 (ANF 5) (New York: Scribner's, 1911), 496–507, 507–557.

Deuteronomy are collected without any headings or commentary.[14] Dating perhaps to the early fifth century, the *Testimonies Against the Jews* attributed to Gregory of Nyssa presents biblical excerpts under such headings as "concerning the unbelief of the Jews and concerning the church of the Gentiles." Most of the excerpts in this last work come from the prophetic books, including the Psalms, and are labeled with the names of the prophets who spoke them (David, Jeremiah, Micah, and so on).[15]

The two Latin anthologies attributed to Cyprian provide the closest analogies to *Talking Back* in terms of both form and function.[16] In each case the author introduces the collection with a prologue that states the overall theme of the book and explains why the author has found it useful to collect the excerpts. Biblical passages are collected under headings such as, "That they [the Jews] should lose Jerusalem and leave the land that they had received," and, "That people are tried by God for this purpose, that they may be proved."[17] The biblical book from which each excerpt is taken is identified. In the prologue to *To Fortunatus*, Cyprian presents martyrdom as Evagrius does monasticism in the prologue to *Talking Back*: it is a war with Satan, in which Christians are "soldiers of Christ," armed with the collected passages from the Bible as their

---

[14] *P. Ryl. Gk.* 460; ed. C. H. Roberts, *Two Biblical Papyri in the John Rylands Library, Manchester* (Manchester: Manchester University Press, 1936), 47–62; cf. Albl, *"And Scripture Cannot Be Broken,"* 139.

[15] Pseudo-Gregory of Nyssa, *Testimonies against the Jews,* Writings from the Greco-Roman World 8, trans. Martin C. Albl (Atlanta: Society of Biblical Literature, 2004); cf. Albl, *"And Scripture Cannot Be Broken,"* 142–44.

[16] Scholars accept cyprianic authorship of *To Fortunatus,* but most doubt that Cyprian wrote *To Quirinus,* although some are open to the possibility that he compiled the third book and not the first two. Even if Cyprian did not compile *To Quirinus,* he appears to have known and made use of it. See Charles A. Bobertz, "'For the Vineyard of the Lord of Hosts was the House of Israel': Cyprian of Carthage and the Jews," *Jewish Quarterly Review* 82 (1991): 1–15, esp. 3–5, and "An Analysis of *Vita Cypriani* 3.6-10 and the Attribution of *Ad Quirinum* to Cyprian of Carthage," *Vigiliae Christianae* 46 (1992): 112–28. For our purposes, this question is not significant.

[17] Cyprian, *Ad Quirinum,* 1.6; CCSL 3/1:11; ANF 5:510; 3.15; CCSL 3/1:106; ANF 5:537.

defensive weapons. *To Quirinus* now consists of three books, but its first two books appear to have been originally separate from the third: one prologue introduces Books 1 and 2, the testimonies of which concern the unbelief of the Jews and the career of Christ, and a second prologue precedes Book 3, which collects passages that promote the proper Christian life. While the first two books, like *To Fortunatus*, anticipate *Talking Back*'s combative or defensive use, the third book of *To Quirinus* parallels *Talking Back*'s less polemical function of building up the reader's character and serving as a means of reading Scripture. The compiler calls Book 3 "a succinct course of sacred reading, so that your [Quirinus's] mind, given over to God, might not be fatigued by long or numerous volumes of books, but, instructed with a summary of heavenly precepts, might have a wholesome and large compendium for nourishing its memory."[18] In his prologue, Evagrius does not likewise present his anthology as a kind of abridged version of the Bible for rapid reading, but Evagrius concludes his letter to Loukios by highlighting the general benefit of "reading the divine Scriptures," which "removes even the love for representations by transferring it [the mind] to the formless, divine, and simple knowledge" (*Ep.* 4.5). *Talking Back*, then, resembles other ancient anthologies of biblical excerpts not only in its literary form, but also in its functions of arming the Christian for spiritual struggle with Satan or polemical conflict with opponents, exhorting the Christian to a higher moral life, and providing an alternative means of reading the Scriptures. At least Gennadius saw the connection when he called *Talking Back* a collection of "testimonies from the holy Scriptures."

Another type of anthology to which *Talking Back* may be compared in both form and function is the "notebook" (usually in the plural, *hupomnēmata*: "notes, reminders") that the cultivated person might compile in the effort to improve himself in virtue. For example, in a situation that anticipates Evagrius's correspondence with Loukios, Plutarch wrote to his friend Paccius, "Just now

---

[18] Cyprian, *Ad Quirinum,* 3. Pref; CCSL 3/1:72; ANF 5:528.

I received your letter, in which you urged me to write for you
something on tranquility of mind and on the things in the *Timaeus*
[of Plato] that require more careful explication." Plutarch professed
to have no time to compose a polished work; instead, "I have collected [excerpts] about tranquility of mind from the notebook
that I happen to have made for myself, supposing that you seek
this treatise, not because you want to hear an elegant composition,
but for practical help."[19] The work that Plutarch sent to Paccius is
indeed full of excerpts and anecdotes that he might have gathered
in a notebook as an aid to his own efforts at cultivating a tranquil
disposition. Occasionally Plutarch directs a quotation at people
with a specific problematic view of the good life; for example, he
considers an excerpt from Menander to be an appropriate cor-
rection for "those who suppose that one form of life is especially
free of pain, as some think concerning the life of farmers or un-
married people or kings."[20] Evagrius directs some of his biblical
excerpts to monks who hold incorrect ideas about the ascetic life
or demonic conflict: such entries begin, "Against the soul that
supposes that . . ."

Michel Foucault drew attention to notebooks such as the one
that Plutarch compiled as an important tool that cultivated persons
of antiquity used for "the shaping of the self."[21] In his analysis,
Foucault emphasized the self-formative function of this kind of
writing: the compilation of the notebook was itself an exercise in
identifying and gathering the best of what one had read or heard;
the writer then sought to unify in his own identity and rational
action the inevitably "disparate" elements that he had collected
from others. One may compare this self-forming literary practice
with Athanasius of Alexandria's description of the young ascetic
Antony observing the diverse virtues manifested in more advanced
ascetics: Antony then "gathered into himself the virtues of each

---

[19] Plutarch, *De tranquillitate animi,* 464e–f.
[20] Plutarch, *De tranquillitate animi,* 466a.
[21] Michel Foucault, "SelfWriting," in Michel Foucault, *Ethics: Subjectivity and
Truth,* The Essential Works of Michel Foucault, 1954–1984, ed. Paul Rabinow,
207–22 (NewYork:The New Press, 1994), quotation at 211.

and strove to display them in himself."[22] Athanasius later has Antony recommend to monks a mode of writing that will develop their character: he suggests that the monk write down "the deeds and movements of [his] soul" as if they were to be read by other monks; in this way, Antony says, the monks will "form themselves."[23] Foucault, however, contrasted the appropriation to oneself of recollected, disparate truths through notebooks with the kind of "narrative of the self" that Athanasius has Antony recommend that Christian monks write, that is, "the oral or written confession [of one's own failings] . . . which has a purificatory value."[24]

Foucault's analysis has drawn criticism, especially of its suggestion of an aesthetic, past-oriented self-fashioning on the part of men such as Plutarch and Seneca, but his argument that the notebook writer "constitutes his own identity through his recollection of things" that others have said seems to characterize also one of the functions of *Talking Back* for its monastic reader.[25] In this case, the monk is not the writer or compiler of the notebook as Plutarch is—it is Evagrius who makes the notebook—but he does shape his self, referred to in *Talking Back* as "the soul" or "the intellect," in part through the recollection and recitation of what others have said in the Bible. He appropriates the collected and disparate sayings to himself as the enunciations for diverse circumstances of a single "monastic life" (Prol.6). In this respect, *Talking Back* resembles the *hupomnēmata* of Foucault's Roman philosophers more than it does the Christian genre of self-confession of which Athanasius's Antony speaks.

Talking Back, however, differs from most other anthologies, including the Christian testimony books and the philosophical *hupomnēmata*, in that many of the excerpts that it collects are meant to be addressed neither to other people nor to oneself, but to

---

[22] Athanasius, *Life of Antony* 4.2.

[23] Athanasius, *Life of Antony* 55.7–13.

[24] Foucault, "Self Writing," 209–14.

[25] Criticism: Pierre Hadot, "Reflections on the Idea of the 'Cultivation of the Self,'" in Pierre Hadot, *Philosophy as a Way of Life*, ed. Arnold I. Davidson, 206–13 (Oxford: Blackwell, 1995). Quotation: Foucault, "Self Writing," 213.

supramundane beings: God, demons, even angels. As an arsenal of effective words to oppose demons, to enlist divine aid, or to help persons in distress, it invites comparison also with the magician's spell manual. Some examples of this genre that survive from late ancient Egypt provide a single prayer that invokes a divine, angelic, or demonic power and follow it with a catalogue of situations in which the prayer may be used and directions as to how to apply the prayer to each case. For example, a Coptic ritual that may date to the fourth or fifth century sets forth a lengthy prayer to God ("O God, O Lord, O Lord, O Omnipotent . . .") and then gives a list of situations in which it can be used, ranging from medical conditions to social problems. Here are some examples:

> For the sting of an insect:
> Recite it over some water, and have him drink it. . . .
> For your enemies, that they may not prevail against you:
> Recite it over some water, adjuring him, and sprinkle your house and every one of your ways. . . .
> For the rescue of ships at sea or on the ocean along with everything:
> Write it upon a clean piece of papyrus, and tie it to the tip of the mast. . . .
> To make someone desire you:
> Recite it over an *aparche* of wine. Give it to him to drink.[26]

Like *Talking Back*, this and similar ritual handbooks address a wide range of concerns, list problematic situations or desired outcomes with brief remedies, and use powerful words to address God, angels, or demons. In contrast to *Talking Back*, however, these rituals (or at least the ones that I have studied) tend to use the same prayer for every situation: either the actions performed or the substances

---

[26] *Michigan Papyrus* 593; ed. and trans. W. H. Worrell, "A Coptic Wizard's Hoard," *American Journal of Semitic Languages and Literatures* 46 (1930): 239–62. It appears also as No. 133 in Marvin Meyer and Richard Smith, eds., *Ancient Christian Magic: Coptic Texts of Ritual Power* (San Francisco: HarperSanFrancisco, 1994), 304–10. For rituals with similar lists of situations, see nos. 128 and 135 in Meyer and Smith, *Ancient Christian Magic*, 270–73, 326–41.

used or both are what vary. With a few exceptions, Evagrius does not advise that the monk perform specific physical actions in the situations that he lists, only that he use the most effective words from the Scriptures. While the "magical" texts combine powerful words, actions, and substances, Evagrius places anti-demonic power fully in the biblical words that he gives to the monk.

Is it possible that Evagrius himself saw his work as an alternative to such ritual handbooks? Athanasius of Alexandria's *Epistle to Marcellinus* suggests that he may have done so. This letter serves as an especially apt analogy for *Talking Back* because it lies close to the monastic tradition of *antirrhēsis*, as I shall discuss shortly. Athanasius suggests the recitation of certain Psalms to address particular conditions in which Christians may find themselves, including persecution, the desire to give thanks to God, and attacks from demons. The words stabilize the soul through a power based in Christ's incarnation. Athanasius explicitly contrasts the effective nature of the words of Scripture with the impotence of magical spells. In ancient Israel, he explains (somewhat anachronistically), people "drove demons away and refuted the plots they directed against human beings merely by reading the Scriptures." But in recent days certain people have "abandoned" the Bible and instead have "composed for themselves plausible words from external sources, and with these have called themselves exorcists." Athanasius says that the demons "mock" persons who use such nonbiblical words; in contrast, those who use passages from the Bible send the demons away in terror because "the Lord is in the words of the Scriptures."[27] The spell-like form of *Talking Back* may have contributed to the efforts of leaders like Athanasius to encourage Christian monks to be less like "magicians" by addressing supramundane beings like God and the demons with scriptural passages rather than with formulae that they had composed themselves or had purchased from ritual specialists.

Talking Back may strike the modern reader as an odd sort of book, but ancient readers probably saw its affinities with several

[27] Athanasius, *Epistle to Marcellinus* 33.

kinds of ancient literary works, including Scripture testimony books, philosophical notebooks, even magicians' handbooks. As diverse as these genres are, they share a recognition of the power of words, whether that power is used to refute enemies, to shape the virtuous self, to invoke divine or supramundane beings—or, as in the case of *Talking Back*, to do all these things. And all of these genres are practical: these books were meant to be used, not just read. It seems unlikely that Evagrius expected many ordinary monks to have copies of *Talking Back*; rather, its entries directed to the struggling soul or intellect suggest that its ideal user is the advanced monk who serves as a guide or spiritual director to other monks. In his letter to Loukios, Evagrius addresses this recipient of a copy of *Talking Back* as such a monastic guide—even of himself. "Be for me," Evagrius asks Loukios, "a preacher of continence, a listener of humility, and a destroyer 'of thoughts and of every proud obstacle that is raised against the knowledge of Christ' [2 Cor 10:4-5]" (*Ep.* 4.2). Loukios must not "hesitate . . . to converse with the brothers" (*Ep.* 4.3). *Talking Back* is meant for someone like Loukios, a monastic authority, who will give to monks under his care the verses appropriate to their particular situations, guiding them in the art of *antirrhēsis*.

The Theory and Practice of Antirrhēsis

Just as Evagrius's *Praktikos* concerns *praktikē*, the practice of the ascetic life, so too *Antirrhētikos* concerns *antirrhēsis*, the practice of talking back. In an excellent study of the Psalms and prayer in Evagrius's spirituality, Luke Dysinger provides a description of the diverse aspects of monastic *antirrhēsis*, which means "refutation" or "contradiction":

> In the practice of *antirrhesis* select biblical verses are employed to counteract the particular *logismos* [thought] against which the monk is struggling. *Antirrhesis* entails the deployment of biblical texts not only against the demons and their *logismoi* [thoughts], but also against sinful tendencies within the self, and even more broadly as "refutations" of particular groups of people and forms of behaviour. Furthermore, antirrhetic

biblical texts may console the tempted soul and remind it of virtues opposed to the *logismoi*. Finally, *antirrhesis* also includes the offering to God of successful biblical prayers.[28]

Whether the monk uses biblical passages negatively, to refute a demon or thought, or positively, to petition God or console a fellow monk, warfare with the demons remains the context for *antirrhēsis*. Thus, its basic character is oppositional as well as verbal—the monk *speaks* the biblical text in the context of *warfare* with the demonic—as the English phrase "talking back" seeks to capture.

The following statistics concerning the addresses of the biblical excerpts in *Talking Back* illustrate both the diversity of *antirrhēsis* and its primarily adversarial character:

1. Excerpts directed against demons or the thoughts they suggest: 315 (63.3%)

    a. Against thoughts: 278 (55.8%)

    b. Against demons: 37 (7.4%)[29]

2. Excerpts directed against a human soul or intellect captive to or at risk from the demons and their thoughts: 134 (26.9%)

    a. Against the soul: 114 (22.9%)

    b. Against the intellect: 20 (4.0%)

3. Excerpts directed to the Lord or the angels: 48 (9.6%)

    a. To the Lord: 46 (9.2%)

    b. To the angel(s): 2 (0.4%)

4. Excerpt concerning a topic: 1 (0.2%)[30]

---

[28] Luke Dysinger, *Psalmody and Prayer in the Writings of Evagrius Ponticus*, Oxford Theological Monographs (Oxford: Oxford University Press, 2005), 132.

[29] Included in this reckoning is 5.17, which is directed "against the anger that . . ."

[30] "Concerning the suffering that comes from temptations" (4.69). My statistics differ from those of Dysinger (*Psalmody and Prayer*, 137). Although some of these differences may be attributed to Dysinger's mistaken view that there are 492 excerpts, I am not able to explain them fully.

Although only 37 of 498 excerpts are directed explicitly against demons, more than half address the thoughts that the demons suggest; that is, they repel the arrows that the demons hurl against the monk (Prol.2). Evagrius frequently identifies thoughts by their demonic instigators—"against the thought of vainglory that . . .", "against the thoughts of listlessness that . . ."—and thus emphasizes that the thoughts are the means by which the demons attack the monk and not simply (or at all) dispositions of the monk's own soul or intellect. Likewise, the excerpts directed "against the soul" or "against the intellect" most often rebuke or reprimand the monk who has succumbed to or is in danger of succumbing to a demonic suggestion, or they correct the monk who holds a mistaken or dangerous view of the ascetic life; others console or encourage the monk who may be in despair over the difficulty of the battle.[31] Fewer than 10 percent ask God or the angels for help or thank them for assistance they have rendered. In *Talking Back* Evagrius surely seeks constructively to form the monk as a virtuous person, but this self-forming discipline takes place within a determinedly polemical, anti-demonic context, in which the vast majority of excerpts are directed toward agents external to the monk, whether hostile (the demons, armed with thoughts) or supportive (God, assisted by angels).

Evagrius would never claim that he invented *antirrhēsis*; rather, he cites two biblical founders for the practice in the Prologue to *Talking Back* and in other works, David and Jesus, whose precedents earlier monastic teachers transmitted. David's reputation as a

---

[31] Dysinger prefers to translate "*for* a soul" and "*for* a mind" (e.g., Dysinger, *Psalmody and Prayer*, 137, emphasis added). Although this translation may capture a somewhat less adversarial spirit in the use of biblical texts directed toward another monk than in such directed against demons or thoughts, the Syriac text provides no support for such a distinction, using in all these cases the preposition *lwqbl*. In contrast, excerpts directed "*to* the Lord" use *lwt* rather than *lwqbl*. In his translation of the Syriac into Greek, Frankenberg suggests that the Greek *pros* lies behind *lwqbl*, and this hypothesis may find support in the examples from *Scholia on the Psalms* that Dysinger cites (*Psalmody and Prayer*, 144); but Evagrius's quotation of Prov 26:4-5, which urges the hearer not to "answer a fool in proportion to (*pros*) his folly," but rather "in opposition to (*kata*) his folly," may argue for *kata* instead.

warrior against the demons rests on his reputed authorship of the book of Psalms (Prol.6), many of which are directed against the speaker's persecutors and enemies, and on his successful warfare against the Philistines, whom Evagrius equates with the demons (Prol.3).[32] Evagrius refers to "the entire contest of the monastic life, which the Holy Spirit taught David through the Psalms" (Prol.6) and thus places the verbal refutation of the demons at the core of the monastic struggle against vice and for virtue. Jesus' use of biblical verses to respond to the temptations of Satan, found in the Gospels of Matthew and Luke (Matt 4:1–11; Luke 4:1–13), provides the other biblical precedent for *antirrhēsis* that Evagrius cites.[33] He couples "what he [Jesus] did," that is, his practice, with "the rest of all his teaching" (Prol.2): both are gifts of the Savior to Christians. Evagrius identifies "the blessed fathers" as those who handed down *antirrhēsis* from its biblical founders (Prol.6). "Blessed fathers" refers primarily, of course, to the experienced monks such as Macarius the Great and Macarius the Alexandrian whose guidance Evagrius sought when he came to the Egyptian desert, but it may also include Gregory of Nazianzus, Evagrius's teacher in Constantinople. Gregory "planted me," Evagrius wrote elsewhere, and "the holy fathers" of the Egyptian desert "now water me."[34]

Gregory taught that the demons attacked baptized Christians and composed a series of what Dayna Kalleres has called "prayer texts," in which attacking demons are addressed and refuted.[35] In Gregory's view, a "paradoxical fusion" of intelligible and sensory

---

[32] See Dysinger, *Psalmody and Prayer*, 131, where he cites the following references to David the spiritual warrior in Evagrius's works: *Thoughts* 10, 14, 20; *Letters* 11.2; 56.8; *Scholia on Ecclesiastes* 10; *Scholia on Proverbs* 12; *Scholia on the Psalms* 14. For the Philistines as demons, see *Letter* 58.2; *Kephalaia Gnostica* 5.30, 36, 68.

[33] See Gabriel Bunge, *Akedia: La doctrine spirituelle d'Évagre le Pontique sur l'acédie* (Bégrolles-en-Mauges: Abbaye de Bellefontaine, 1991): 111–12.

[34] *Praktikos* Epilogue.

[35] The texts appear in *Patrologia Graeca* 37:1397–1406. Dayna Kalleres has reproduced, translated, and analyzed them in "Demons and Divine Illumination: A Consideration of Certain Prayers by Gregory of Nazianzus," *Vigiliae Christianae* 67 (2007): 157–88. I am grateful to Professor Kalleres for sharing this article with me in advance of publication.

essences in Adam had enabled him to know God, but the fall upset
this balance. Baptism unites a person to Christ, in whom this
paradoxical fusion was restored, and thus sets the baptized Christian on a path toward renewed apprehension and contemplation
of God.[36] Demons attempt to thwart the Christian's progress
toward divine contemplation by introducing false impressions and
images and so distorting proper knowledge. The Christian, then,
must learn to discern, as the Stoics had taught, true and false impressions, but Gregory also composed short prayers that function
as apotropaic speech to repel the demons. For example, one prayer
begins, "You have come, o evil doer, I recognize your thoughts.
You have come, in order that you might deprive me of the light
and beloved life."[37] Here the speaker announces his successful
discernment of a demonic thought. Another prayer simply seeks
to send the demon away:

> Go away, go away, evil one, manslayer;
> Go away, sight of terrible sufferings, raging evil;
> Go away, Christ is within, to whom I have offered
> and given my soul. Flee, giving up as quickly as possible.
> O help, angels stand by!
> O the tyrant, and the thief is approaching.
> From them take me away, yes, beloved ones, I am being stoned.[38]

In this case the presence both of Christ within the baptized Christian and of attendant angels nearby helps to send the demons away.
Other prayers refer to the mark of the cross within the baptized
person. The prayers use speech to harness this divine power against
the demons, and they draw on the rites that attended baptism,
which included exorcisms and verbal renunciations of Satan and

---

[36] See not only Kalleres, "Demons and Divine Illumination," but also Susanna
Elm, "Inscriptions and Conversions: Gregory of Nazianzus on Baptism," in *Con-
version in Late Antiquity and the Early Middle Ages: Seeing and Believing*, ed. A. Grafton
and K. Mills, 1–35 (New York: University of Rochester Press, 2003).

[37] Prayer 1 (Kalleres, "Demons and Divine Illumination," 161–62).

[38] Prayer 5 (Kalleres, "Demons and Divine Illumination," 166).

his demons.[39] It is possible that Gregory composed these anti-demonic prayers after he had left Constantinople for retirement and Evagrius had departed for Jerusalem and the Egypt,[40] but they suggest that Evagrius could have arrived in Egypt already having learned from Gregory about the danger of demonic thoughts and the possibility of refuting them verbally with powerful words. He would, then, have been well prepared for the monastic practice of *antirrhēsis* as taught and performed by the monks he called "the blessed fathers."

One of those "blessed fathers" was Antony. Antony died long before Evagrius became a monk, but Evagrius knew the Antony who appears in Athanasius's *Life of Antony* singing Psalms and reciting biblical verses to repel demons.[41] Verbal give-and-take characterizes Antony's first conflict with the devil, which comes after he has achieved a high level of virtue already as a young man: "The one suggested filthy thoughts, but the other repelled them with prayers."[42] Athanasius does not identify these prayers as scriptural, but the power of biblical verses soon becomes evident when the devil appears to Antony as a black boy. Antony gives a short speech of refutation to the demon, concluding with Psalm 117:7: "The Lord is my helper, and I will look down on my enemies." "When he heard this," Athanasius writes, "the black one immediately fled, cowering before these words and afraid even to approach the man."[43] In Antony's long ascetic discourse to other monks, Athanasius has him say that when "the saints" saw demonic appearances, they recited verses from the Psalms, ironically ones

---

[39] See Henry Ansgar Kelly, *The Devil at Baptism: Ritual, Theology, and Drama* (Ithaca, NY: Cornell University Press, 1985), 81–122, 136–57, and Dayna Kalleres, "Exorcising the Devil to Silence Christ's Enemies: Ritualized Speech Practices in Late Antique Christianity" (PHD dissertation, Brown University, 2002).

[40] Kalleres, "Demons and Divine Illumination," 161n13.

[41] Gabriel Bunge quips, perhaps only half-jokingly, that Evagrius must have known the *Life of Antony* by heart ("Évagre le Pontique et les deux Macaire," *Irénikon* 56 [1983]: 215–27, 323–60, at 332).

[42] Athanasius, *Life of Antony* 5.4.

[43] Athanasius, *Life of Antony* 6.4–5.

that refer to not speaking and keeping one's mouth closed.[44] But
here too the more significant precedent is Jesus' use of biblical
passages to refute Satan's temptations: "For what the Lord said, he
did for our sakes, so that when the demons hear similar such sayings from us they will be overturned because of the Lord, who
rebuked them with these sayings."[45] Note that Athanasius has
Antony attribute the anti-demonic power not to the biblical words
themselves, but to "the Lord," who first used them. This subtle
distinction may not have been clear to every reader of the *Life*,
which frequently portrays Antony singing Psalms or reciting other
biblical verses in his conflicts with demons without such Christological explanations.[46] Antony, of course, uses other means to
repel demons—for example, the sign of the cross, the name of
Christ, and his own words[47]—but biblical verses, especially from
the Psalms, are his most frequent spiritual weapons.

There can be no doubt that Evagrius had read the *Life of Antony*
and appropriated many of its teachings. In *Talking Back* he explicitly invokes the example of Antony: confronted by "the demons
that gradually begin to imitate obscene images and to appear out
of the air," the monk "should answer with a phrase, as also the
righteous blessed Antony answered and said: 'The Lord is my
helper, and I shall look upon my enemies' [Ps 117:7]" (*Ant.* 4.47).
Evagrius cites precisely the verse that Antony uses in the *Life* to
repel the devil's appearance as a black boy. Eight more scriptural
passages in Book 4 appear also in the *Life* as citations or allusions,
most in Antony's ascetic discourse on demons.[48] The predominant
theme of Book 4 on the demon of sadness is the discouragement
or fear that the monk may feel in the face of demonic attacks,

---

[44] Athanasius, *Life of Antony* 27.1–3, citing Pss 38:2–3; 37:14–15.
[45] Athanasius, *Life of Antony* 37.3–4.
[46] Athanasius, *Life of Antony* 9.2–3; 13.7; 39.3; 40.5; 41.5.
[47] Athanasius, *Life of Antony* 35.2; 41.6; 52–53.
[48] Exod 15:9: *Ant.* 4.7, *Life* 24.3. 2 Kgs 6:17: *Ant.* 4.27, *Life* 34.3. Ps 19:8–9:
Ant. 4.32, *Life* 39.3. Ps 26:3: *Ant.* 4.34, *Life* 9.3. Job 1:10–11: *Ant.* 4.51, *Life* 29.3.
Job 2:4–5: *Ant.* 4.52, *Life* 29.1. Matt 8:30–32: *Ant.* 4.66, *Life* 29.5. Rom 8:18: *Ant.*
4.70, *Life* 17.1.

especially those that are visual, physical, or both. The temptation to lose heart in one's battle with the demons, not an important aspect of sadness as Evagrius describes it in his other works, appears prominently in the *Life of Antony*. Athanasius portrays Antony as facing fearsome and painful demonic appearances and yet maintaining his spiritual integrity and faith in God. Here the *Life of Antony* has clearly influenced Evagrius's presentation of monastic spirituality and of *antirrhēsis* in particular.[49]

Athanasius, we have already seen, attributed anti-demonic power to the words of Scripture also in his *Epistle to Marcellinus*: unlike the exorcistic texts that contemporary people compose, "the Lord himself is in the words of the Scriptures," which therefore have the power to drive demons away.[50] This teaching echoes that attributed to Antony in the *Life*. But in his letter to Marcellinus, Athanasius places greater emphasis on the therapeutic value of reciting the Psalms, which he understands to epitomize the entire canon of Scriptures, and thus articulates the self-formative aspect of *antirrhēsis*.[51] The Psalms can help to ameliorate the individual's vulnerability to the passions and form him or her into a virtuous subject thanks to their double character. On the one hand, the Psalms make present Christ's own life, the secure model to which the changeable human being must conform him- or herself; on the other hand, they provide a mirror of the human soul's movements and dispositions. Reciting the Psalms becomes a means of both therapeutic recognition of the soul's condition and ethical formation of the soul after the pattern of Christ.[52] It is arguable that certain excerpts in *Talking Back*, especially those directed to God in the first person, have this same function.[53] It is not clear

---

[49] See Brakke, *Demons and the Making of the Monk*, 23–47, 63–65.

[50] Athanasius, *Epistle to Marcellinus* 33.

[51] See especially Paul R. Kolbet, "Athanasius, the Psalms, and the Reformation of the Self," *Harvard Theological Review* 99 (2006): 85–101.

[52] Kolbet, "Athanasius, the Psalms, and the Reformation," esp. 94–95.

[53] E.g., "To the Lord concerning the thoughts of listlessness that are in us, 'So-and-so, one of our brothers or one of our relatives, has attained and joined a rank of honor and authority, and he has become a powerful man': 'It is good for me to cleave to God, to place my hope in the Lord' [Ps 72:28]" (6.23).

whether Evagrius had read the *Epistle to Marcellinus*, but his statement that "the melody that is applied to the Psalms alters the
condition of the body" (*Ant.* 4.22) may indicate knowledge of the
Epistle's teaching that the melody affects the soul, which can then
bring harmony to the body's members.[54]

The anti-demonic use of scriptural verses appears in the *Sayings
of the Desert Fathers* as well, although often in a way that renders
the biblical character of the words or the precise nature of their
power ambiguous. For example, when the demons ask an old man
(that is, an advanced monk) whether he would like to see Christ,
he anathematizes them and their question, declaring, "I believe in
my Christ, who says, 'If someone says to you, "Look, the Christ is
here or he is there," do not believe' [Matt 24:23]." Immediately
the demons disappear.[55] The story leaves unclear whether it is
specifically the monk's quotation of Matthew or his general rebuke
that repels the demons. When a monk plagued by thoughts of
blasphemy asks him for advice, Poemen recommends a refuting
statement that is not biblical.[56] According to another anecdote, a
monk troubled by thoughts of fornication asked a more senior
monk for advice:

> The brother answered and said, "What shall I do, for I am
> weak and the passion defeats me?" He [the old man] said,
> "Observe them [the demons], and when they begin to speak,
> do not answer them, but get up, pray, and make repentance,
> saying, 'Son of God, have mercy on me!'" And again the
> brother said, "I recite, Abba, and yet there is no compunction
> in my heart because I do not understand the force of the say-
> ing." And he said to him, "In your case, just recite. For I have
> heard that Abba Poemen and many fathers made this state-
> ment: 'The charmer does not understand the force of the
> words that he says, but the beast hears, understands the force
> of the saying, and submits. So too with us: even if we do not

---

[54] Athanasius, *Epistle to Marcellinus* 28.
[55] *Apophthegmata Patrum* 15.90 (= N 313).
[56] *Apophthegmata Patrum* 10.63; cf. Poemen 93.

understand the force of the things we say, when the demons hear, they withdraw in fear.'"[57]

The words that the monk speaks have such power that the speaker need not understand their "force," that is, both their meaning and their effectiveness, for them to repel the demons. Still, the words that the story recommends—"Son of God, have mercy on me"— are not precisely scriptural, although they may allude to such passages as Matthew 9:27, and in any event the story does not attribute their power to their possible biblical origins. The *Sayings of the Desert Fathers* provide evidence for such monastic practices of *antirrhēsis* as short prayers offered to God and rebuking state- ments aimed at demons or thoughts, but unlike Athanasius and Evagrius, they do not insist on the use of biblical verses in such speech.

Our anecdote from the *Sayings* characterizes the power of the monk's anti-demonic words as similar to that of magical spells, as a quality that is inherent in the words themselves, while Athanasius attributed the effectiveness to Jesus ("the Lord"), who originally used biblical words to refute Satan and who makes himself present in the Psalms. Evagrius would probably not deny either of these views, but he presented his own theory of why *antirrhēsis* works, which reflects his well-developed understanding of how the human intellect works. In the prologue to *Talking Back*, he cites Qoheleth: "No refutation [*antirrhēsis*] comes from those who per- form evil quickly; therefore, the heart of the children of humanity has become confirmed with them for the doing of evil" (8:11). Evagrius interprets this and related verses (Ezek 18:4; Prov 26:4-5) to mean that one should refute an evil thought as soon as possible after it occurs to one, before "it is firmly set in one's thinking"; if the monk does so, "sin is easily and swiftly handled." But if the thought is allowed to persist, it leads the soul from merely thinking about sin to actually performing sin and thus to death (Prol.2). By repelling the evil thought, *antirrhēsis* prevents the monk from per- forming the evil deed.

---

[57] *Apophthegmata Patrum* 5.37 (= N 184).

Evagrius inherited the idea behind this practice from his predecessor Origen (ca. 185–254) and his contemporary Didymus the Blind (ca. 313–98), both of whom adapted to Christian ethics the Stoic notion of a "proto-passion" (*propatheia*) or "first movement."[58] In the Stoic view morally culpable passions such as anger or lust result from our making poor judgments and assenting to an impulse or impression beyond what is natural or reasonable. All people are subject to involuntary "first movements," which we may either control and use to good ends or allow to develop into a morally culpable passion. For example, I may have a visceral rush of anger when I learn of some injustice (first movement), but I can control it and respond appropriately by, say, calmly rebuking the offender. But if I assent to the impulse unreasonably and allow the full-blown passion of anger to develop, then I become guilty of the passion. First movements may come from the movements of the body (for example, the sexual urge), but they may also arise as responses to external stimuli (for example, the news of some injustice), which Stoics sometimes called "impressions" (*phantasiai*). The Stoics argued that we encounter a wide range of impressions, incoming images and ideas, which we must sort out as true or false, leading to virtue or vice, and the like. However a first movement arises, it is the person's rational faculty, the intellect, that forms a judgment about the movement and either arrests it or allows it to develop into a full-fledged passion.

Origen and Didymus took over this teaching and adapted it to Christian views, in which Satan could serve as an external source for such first movements. One motivation to do so was exegetical: the notion of an involuntary and morally innocent "proto-passion" could explain, for example, biblical passages that appeared to attribute emotions to Jesus or other virtuous persons.

[58] On this topic see Richard Sorabji, *Emotion and Peace of Mind: From Stoic Agitation to Christian Temptation* (Oxford: Oxford University Press, 2000); Margaret R. Graver, *Stoicism and Emotion* (Chicago and London: University of Chicago Press, 2007), 85–108; Richard Layton, "Propatheia: Origen and Didymus on the Origin of the Passions," *Vigiliae Christianae* 54 (2000): 262–82; Brakke, *Demons and the Making of the Monk*, 38–41, 54–56.

The Jewish Alexandrian scholar Philo (d. ca. 45 CE) had already used this strategy in his exegesis of the Septuagint. Origen and Didymus applied the idea to the Christian's conflict with Satan and the demons as well. Origen used the technical term "first movements" (*primi motus*) to refer to impulses that arise from the body ("according to the desire of the flesh"), which the soul can either bring under control or allow to develop into sin. Demons can incite to greater sin the soul that fails to stop a first movement.[59] Without calling them "first movements," Origen also called attention to thoughts that come from demons and incite us to evil deeds; we cannot help but receive such thoughts, but we can choose whether to resist or act upon them. He cited Satan's suggestion of betrayal to Judas—the devil "cast" the idea "into his heart," according to John 13:2—as an example of a demonically inspired thought that a person could have resisted.[60] Such thoughts function like the Stoics' impressions. Didymus likewise cited the example of Judas, but he called Satan's suggestion a "first movement" (*propatheia*): rather than rejecting it immediately, Judas allowed the first movement to persist and to become a full-fledged passion and then a disposition of the soul, which led him to commit the evil act.[61]

Evagrius's teaching stands in this tradition of Christian appropriation of Stoic ideas. According to Evagrius, the monk must, like the Stoic sage, exercise discernment in sorting through the thoughts and images that confront him. He writes to Loukios:

> When the battle takes place with discernment, it is filled with many thoughts, but it creates a great purity of thinking because the demons can no longer mock or accuse the soul. For just as practical wisdom is assigned the reasonable judgment of practical matters, so too discernment is entrusted with the impressions [*phantasiai*] that occur in thinking,

---

[59] Origen, *On First Principles* 3.2.2; *Homilies on Exodus* 4.8.

[60] Origen, *On First Principles* 3.2.4.

[61] Didymus the Blind, *Commentary on Ecclesiastes* 294.8-20. See Richard A. Layton, *Didymus the Blind and his Circle in Late-Antique Alexandria: Virtue and Narrative in Biblical Scholarship* (Urbana: University of Illinois Press, 2004), 117–29.

discerning holy and profane, clean and unclean thoughts. And, according to the prophetic saying, it [discernment] has experience of the tricks of the mocking demons, which imitate both perception and memory in order to deceive the rational soul that strives for the knowledge of Christ (*Ep.* 4.4).

The first step in *antirrhēsis*, then, is to identify an impression as a demonic thought, a task that requires the gift of discernment.[62] Even if correctly identified, an evil thought can still function like a first movement, inciting us to sin. A demon presents an evil thought to us, and we have the power to put a stop to it. If we do not, but instead allow it to persist, it will lead us into evil action. *Talking Back*'s arsenal of biblical verses provides a means for preventing a demonically inspired first movement from developing into a full-fledged passion and thus into sin. Evagrius was not unique in adapting to Christian spiritual warfare such ethical perspectives and therapeutic speech practices from philosophical traditions: John Chrysostom did so as well in his recommendations to newly baptized Christians and their sponsors.[63]

But the goal of the Evagrian monk is not simply to avoid evil deeds; remarkably, he seeks not to experience the first movements that incite to sin at all. Evagrius urges his reader to become not merely a "monastic man," that is, someone who has withdrawn from committing sins in action, but rather, a "monastic intellect," that is, someone who is free even from thoughts of sin. Such a thought-free monk enjoys complete clarity of mind and "at the time of prayer sees the light of the Holy Trinity" (Prol.5). The ultimate goal is to eliminate the thoughts themselves and to pray and contemplate God purely. The biblical verses he provides in this book are designed, as he puts it, to "cut off" their corresponding thoughts (Prol.6).

---

[62] On discernment in Evagrius, see Antony D. Rich, *Discernment in the Desert Fathers: 'Diakrisis' in the Life and Thought of Early Egyptian Monasticism*, Studies in Christian History and Thought (Milton Keyes, U.K.: Paternoster, 2007), 39–74.

[63] Kalleres, "Exorcising the Devil to Silence Christ's Enemies," 93–98.

With the use of the term "cut off" Evagrius alludes to his theory of mental operations, which lies behind his concept of *antirrhēsis* but which he does not explain fully in *Talking Back*. In his treatise *Thoughts* Evagrius provides a more thorough explanation of this "cutting off":

> Among the thoughts some cut off, and others are cut off: the evil thoughts cut off the good ones, and likewise the evil thoughts are cut off by the good ones. And so the Holy Spirit pays attention to the thought that is given priority, and it condemns us or approves of us based on that. What I am saying is like this: I have a certain thought concerning hospitality, and I have it for the sake of the Lord, but this thought is cut off when the tempter attacks and suggests that I show hospitality for the sake of glory. Likewise I have a thought that I should manifest hospitality before human beings, but this thought too is cut off when a better thought intervenes that directs our virtue toward the Lord instead and dissuades us from practicing it for the sake of human beings. Therefore, should we, through our actions, finally stick with the prior thoughts, despite being tested by the second ones, we shall receive only the reward that belongs to the thoughts that are given priority. Because we are human beings and wrestlers with demons, we cannot always keep the proper thought uncorrupted, nor conversely can we hold the evil thought untested since we possess seeds of virtues. But if one of the thoughts that cut off persists, it settles itself in the place of cutting off, and eventually the person will be set in motion by that thought and become active.[64]

This passage provides the broader context for *antirrhēsis*. Every thought that we have, good or bad, can be cut off by a corresponding opposing thought, and in fact Evagrius suggests that nearly every thought that we have does encounter its opposite. The question is whether we stick with the first thought despite the challenge of the second or whether the first thought is cut off and the second

---

[64] *Thoughts* 7; this discussion appears also in Letter 18.3–5.

persists and sets us on a course of action. In Evagrius's view the
conflict between thoughts within the intellect is endemic to the
fallen human condition: we may still possess "seeds of virtues," but
we are human beings, not angels, and so "wrestlers with demons."
In *antirrhēsis*, then, the monk deliberately sets in motion a process
that would otherwise take place inevitably by consciously using
good thoughts drawn from the Bible to cut off bad ones suggested
by the demons. *Antirrhēsis* works because it corresponds with how
the fallen human intellect works.

It should be noted, however, that in *Thoughts* Evagrius gives
three sources for the good thoughts that might cut off demonic
ones, and these do not include the Bible. He writes:

> Three thoughts oppose the demonic thought, cutting it off
> when it persists in one's thinking: the angelic thought; the
> thought that arises from our free will when it inclines toward
> the better; and the thought that is imparted naturally by our
> humanity, which sets even the pagans in motion to love their
> children and honor their parents. Only two thoughts oppose
> the good thought: the demonic thought and the thought that
> arises from our free will when it declines toward the worse.
> No evil thought comes from our nature, for we have not been
> evil from our origin, since it is good seed that the Lord sowed
> in his field [cf. Matt 13:24].[65]

One might argue that biblical verses might be included in the
category of angelic thoughts, but it seems more honest to set the
biblical thoughts of *Talking Back* alongside the angelic thoughts
mentioned here as opposing thoughts that come to the monk
from outside himself. In any event, Evagrius indicates that he
understands the biblical passages in these terms when in the Prologue he uses the technical term "cut off" to describe their effect
on demonic thoughts.

Persistent evil thoughts, ones that are not cut off by good
thoughts, pose great danger to the monk: not only do they set him

---

[65] *Thoughts* 31; this discussion appears also in *Letter* 18.1–2; cf. *Reflections* 46.

in motion to sin in deed, but they distort his intellect and prevent him from achieving knowledge of God or seeing the light of the Trinity in prayer.[66] Here we may see a more direct debt to Gregory of Nazianzus's teachings about demons and divine illumination that I discussed above. According to Evagrius, thoughts have some (usually propositional) content (such as, "I should store up more bread") and can come from angels (good), demons (bad), or the monk himself (good, bad, or neutral). But thoughts make use of the more basic intellectual material of representations (*noēmata*), which are simple concepts that Evagrius understands primarily in visual terms (for instance, the image of bread). Representations come to us through the body's senses, but they can be stored in memory and thus retrieved by the intellect or by the demons even while the monk is asleep and his body inactive. The mind cannot think without representations: even the thoughts of hospitality that Evagrius mentioned above require some representation, perhaps an image of the food that the monk would offer his guest. Representations themselves are neither good nor bad—they are like sheep, given to the intellect to shepherd responsibly—but they serve as the basis for thoughts, which can be morally evaluated. For example, the representation of gold has no moral significance, but thoughts about gold do. The angelic thought that leads the monk to consider why gold was created and what it symbolizes in the Bible is good, whereas the demonic thought that suggests acquiring gold is bad, enflaming the passion of love of money.

The close connection between thoughts and representations means that persistent thoughts cause representations to persist in the intellect. The intellect can entertain only one representation at a time, but representations often move through the intellect at a rapid pace, giving the illusion of simultaneity. A representation can persist in the intellect if a bad thought, one that enflames a passion, attaches to it (an "impassioned" representation); the representation of gold, for instance, persists in the intellect of the

[66] For the following two paragraphs, see *Thoughts* 2, 4, 8, 17, 22, 24, 25, 32, 36, 41; Columba Stewart, "Imageless Prayer and the Theological Vision of Evagrius Ponticus," *Journal of Early Christian Studies* 9 (2001): 173–204, esp. 186–89.

greedy person. A persistent representation of a corporeal object can "imprint" the intellect, distorting the intellect in a way that prevents the clarity of vision required for knowledge of God and pure prayer.[67] Evagrius alludes to this phenomenon in *Talking Back* when he describes how the thoughts of a resentful soul can leave the intellect "enflamed with anger" so that, "even after the thought of this passion subsides and some time has passed, there remains a representation of a word or transitory matter that clouds and imprints the intellect" (5.21). Likewise, regretting the alms that one has given to the poor causes thoughts about money to persist and harm the intellect (3.47). Persistent bad thoughts, then, not only lead the monk into sin, but also, by causing impassioned representations to persist in the intellect, damage the intellect, preventing the monk from becoming the "monastic intellect" that sees the light of the Trinity at the time of prayer.

The practice of *antirrhēsis* that *Talking Back* facilitates not only belongs to the first stage in Evagrius's view of the monastic life, ascetic practice (*praktikē*), in which the monk battles the demons and the vices and acquires the virtues; it applies also to the more advanced stage of the monastic "gnostic" (*gnōstikos*), in which the monk contemplates the material world and rational beings on his path to knowledge of God. Demonic suggestions, especially of vainglory and pride, continue to plague the gnostic monk, and the practices of biblical refutation and short prayers to God help to clear his intellect of evil thoughts and distorting representations and thus to prepare him for the vision of the Trinity's light.

Monastic Authority: Evagrius the Fighter of Demons

These comments have focused on the function of *Talking Back* for the reader, its user, so to speak, but have not considered the role of the compiler. By what authority does Evagrius compose a work like *Talking Back*? How does the work configure the legitimacy of its author and thus its reliability in the monk's conflict with the

---

[67] See *Thoughts* 22, 41; *Reflections* 23; *Chapters on Prayer* 55–57, 67–68, 70.

demons? *Talking Back* invites such questions not only because all such works do but also because the author's voice appears most fully only in the Prologue and surfaces only indirectly or sporadically in the remainder of the work. Leaving aside the question of Evagrius's authority generally within late fourth-century monasticism, we can identify at least three ways in which *Talking Back* legitimates Evagrius as an expert in demonic combat: it presents Evagrius as an experienced and successful fighter with demons, an heir to a long tradition of monastic teachers, and a perceptive reader of the Scriptures.

Evagrius's firsthand experience of demonic combat forms the primary source of his authority here: it is this experience to which Loukios appeals in his letter requesting the work. Evagrius, Loukios claims, has lived in the desert a long time, and he is at home there ("as if at a mother's breast"); he has achieved such a level of success in his contests with the demons that the demons fear him and he has summoned others to take up the fight. It is because Evagrius has personal knowledge of the demons and the combat with them, not because he is learned, that Loukios seeks a treatise from him. This picture of Evagrius remained influential in early monasticism even after Evagrius's death: Palladius noted that Evagrius received the gift of discerning spirits, and he vividly described Evagrius's physical and mental conflicts with demons.[68] While students of Evagrius, whether ancient or modern, have noted both his education in philosophy or theology and his experience in demonic combat, it may be argued that his modern interpreters have stressed the former and neglected the latter to an extent that his ancient colleagues would not.[69]

Evagrius himself does not invoke his personal experience as directly or primarily as Loukios does, but it nonetheless functions as a powerful form of self-legitimation in *Talking Back*. In his reply to Loukios, which functions as a cover letter for *Talking Back*, Evagrius confesses to not having dealt with demonic attacks as

---

[68] Palladius, *Lausiac History* 38.10–12.

[69] For an example of an ancient observer who notes both Evagrius's learning and his experience with demons, see *Historia Monachorum* 20.15–16.

well as he should have and remarks that he has suffered greatly because of the demons since Loukios left him. He adduces his experience with severe demonic conflict without explicitly claiming any success in it; instead, he praises God for what he has learned of Loukios's asceticism (*Ep.* 4.1). This self-presentation resembles the opening of *Letter* 55, in which Evagrius calls himself "full of passions" and "a coward." Robin Darling Young suggests that in *Letter* 55 Evagrius "presents himself as nonauthoritative and even fearful, perhaps in order to gain the confidence of his addressee, perhaps as part of his own strategy in the monastic combat against thoughts and their prompting demons who, once they saw signs of arrogance instead of humility, engaged in battle to bring down the monastic teacher."[70] Both motivations seem likely to be in play here, as Evagrius expresses solidarity with Loukios and embodies the humility that repels demons, but certainly his reference to the "unspeakable sufferings" that the demons have inflicted on him also represents a subtle claim to authority.

In the Prologue to *Talking Back*, Evagrius does not refer to his own experience, but rather highlights his reception of monastic tradition, to which I shall turn next. Still, in the subsequent eight books he does frequently signal to the reader his firsthand acquaintance with the demons and their tricks. At the most basic level, the frequent use of the first person ("me," "us") as the recipient of thoughts or the object of demonic attacks places the author among those who have experienced these things. But some of these references appear too specific to Evagrius's own situation to be taken as merely the report of experiences that are simply typical or that belong only to others; among these I include the threat that the monk will experience shame for revealing "all the kinds of all the unclean thoughts" (4.25). As evidence for the sometimes fantastic things that he reports, Evagrius can appeal to his firsthand visual confirmation (2.65; 4.36) and to the knowledge of monks

[70] Robin Darling Young, "Cannibalism and Other Family Woes in Letter 55 of Evagrius of Pontus," in *The World of Early Egyptian Christianity: Language, Literature, and Social Context,* ed. James E. Goehring and Janet A. Timbie, 130–39 (Washington: The Catholic University of America Press, 2007), at 135.

who have undergone such experiences: "those who have been tempted by this demon will understand what I am saying" (2.55; cf. 8.21). His explicit refusals to describe certain experiences in writing because of their disturbing quality alert the reader that Evagrius knows even more than the work itself contains and thus more than even the most attentive reader who has not had experiences like his (2.65; 8.21). At one point Evagrius rebukes critics who "ridicule" accounts of demonic attack as persons who lack experience (4.72), and his condemnations of certain seemingly positive visions (of God or Christ) as the products of the demons of vainglory or pride serve to label the visionary experiences of other monks as illegitimate (7.31; 8.17, 21). He may not say so explicitly, but Evagrius indicates that he is a veteran spiritual warrior, with longer and better experiences of demonic combat than others.

Evagrius more explicitly invests authority in the monastic tradition that he has inherited from older monks and that he claims to be transmitting. In the Prologue, as we have seen, he professes not to present a new program for the ascetic life, but only to make more accessible a very ancient tradition: "I have made public the entire contest of the monastic life, which the Holy Spirit taught David through the Psalms and the blessed fathers handed over to us, but which I have named in this book after these [demons]" (Prol.6). The only innovation that Evagrius makes is to organize this presentation of the monastic life by the named demons. Here he refers only in general to "the blessed fathers" as the immediate sources of his teaching, but he later mentions three of his teachers by name: John of Lycopolis, whom he calls "the seer [or prophet] of Thebes" (2.36; 5.6; 6.16; 7.19), Macarius the Alexandrian (4.23, 58; 8.26), and Macarius the Egyptian or the Great (4.45).[71] John appears as an authority on the workings of the intellect, wise to the demonic images that appear in it (2.36; 5.6) and schooled in what can and cannot be known about its nature (6.16). Each of the four times that he names either Macarius the Alexandrian or

[71] For sorting out the identities of the two Macarii, see Bunge, "Évagre le Pontique et les deux Macaire," 218–23.

Macarius the Great Evagrius cites them as the precedent for using the specific verse in answering back to a demon. In his book *Thoughts*, Evagrius twice mentions Macarius the Alexandrian, who was the priest at Kellia, as an authority on the activities of demons.[72] Although the distinction should not be pressed too far, John appears primarily as a source for theoretical knowledge about the intellect, and the two Macarii for practical knowledge about demonic combat. In any event, these three prominent monks represent specific conduits of the traditions of "the blessed fathers," which Evagrius claims to transmit.

Finally, Evagrius appears as an authoritative reader of the Bible, study of which emerges as an advanced ascetic practice. His mastery appears first in his ability to select "carefully" from the entire Bible the words that are most suited to demonic conflict, even though they are "scattered" and "difficult to find" (Prol.3). His cover letter to Loukios presents *Talking Back* as a particular form of scriptural reading, which purifies the intellect by transferring it from worldly matters to spiritual knowledge. Because other ascetic practices like fasting have the lower aim of eliminating the passions, reading the Scriptures emerges here as a more advanced endeavor, even sequentially following ascetic practice (*Ep.* 4.3–5). Appropriately, then, reading the Scriptures becomes an issue in combat with the final two demons, vainglory and pride, which tempt the monk either to abandon the effort or to accept the demons' own interpretations (7.14; 8.21, 26). Implicitly, throughout *Talking Back*, it is Evagrius who can see the anti-demonic implications of numerous biblical passages that the less advanced reader might never have recognized. For this reason we should not draw a sharp distinction between the allegorical exegesis aimed at contemplation that Evagrius practices in such other works as his exegetical scholia and the *antirrhetic* use of the Bible here: references to the *antirrhetic* functions of biblical passages can be found in the scholia, and the anti-demonic force of some of the passages cited in *Talking Back* can be seen only through figural

---

[72] *Thoughts* 33, 37.

interpretation. The Bible functions diversely at every level of Evagrius's spiritual program.[73]

However Evagrius may have understood his own authority, the publication and dissemination of *Talking Back* in antiquity cemented his reputation as an outstanding opponent of the demons, familiar with their tactics and adept at countering them.

Evidence for Early Monasticism

As fascinating as *Talking Back* is as a window into a crucial aspect of early monastic spirituality, it is of interest also as a source for the lifestyle and experiences of the monks resident in northern Egypt in the late fourth century. To reconstruct early monasticism in Nitria, Scetis, and Kellia, historians have relied primarily on such sources as the *Sayings of the Desert Fathers*, the *History of the Monks of Egypt* (*Historia monachorum*), and Palladius's *Lausiac History*. But these works are not entirely satisfactory: none of them was written in Egypt during the fourth century. Although it can be dated to the 390s, a Palestinian monk composed the *History of the Monks* after he had returned home from a journey among monastic settlements in Egypt. Palladius did live among the monks during this period, but he wrote his account decades later as a bishop in Asia Minor. As we have seen, though, it is possible that the Coptic fragments of Palladian material, including the *Life of Evagrius*, preserve an earlier work of Palladius. And the various collections of the *Sayings*, although they doubtless preserve oral traditions and even reflect smaller written collections from the fourth century, originated no earlier than the second half of the fifth century in Palestine. Historians, then, increasingly question the accuracy of a picture of northern Egyptian monasticism based primarily on these works. It is arguable that some scholars have become too

---

[73] On this point see Dysinger, *Psalmody and Prayer*, esp. 142–49 on antirrhetic texts in the *Scholia on Psalms*. Michael O'Laughlin draws too sharp a contrast in "The Bible, the Demons, and the Desert: Evaluating the *Antirrheticus* of Evagrius Ponticus," *Studia Monastica* 34 (1992): 201–15, at 202–4.

skeptical, especially of the *Sayings*, but there is no denying the shortcomings of these works as historical sources.[74]

Evagrius, in contrast, composed his works while he lived as a monk in Nitria and Kellia. Although most of his works deal with matters of ascetic theory, spirituality, and biblical exegesis and provide few details of monastic social life, *Talking Back* refers constantly to the everyday lives of monks, circumstances that they regularly faced, and the emotions that monks felt. It represents a neglected source for the texture of early monastic life.[75] The monks of Kellia would spend their weeks in solitude but gather on Saturdays and Sundays for shared worship and conversation. The Coptic *Life of Evagrius* reports that these weekly gatherings offered monks the opportunity to consult Evagrius about their struggles with demonic thoughts:

> This was his practice: The brothers would gather around him on Saturday and Sunday, discussing their thoughts with him throughout the night, listening to his words of encouragement until sunrise. And thus they would leave rejoicing and glorifying God, for Evagrius' teaching was very sweet. When they came to see him, he encouraged them, saying to them, "My brothers, if one of you has either a profound or a troubled thought, let him be silent until the brothers depart and let him reflect on it alone with me. Let us not make him speak in front of the brothers lest a little one perish on account of his thoughts and grief swallow him at a gulp."[76]

It seems likely that much of the data found in *Talking Back*, the thoughts that it lists, came from these and other discussions Evagrius had with his fellow monks as well as from his own experience. In any event, this work would be useful to its monastic readers only if it genuinely reflected their experiences. Thus,

---

[74] See my brief discussions of these issues in *Demons and the Making of the Monk*, 127–29, 145–46, with the literature cited there.

[75] See Bunge, "Der Prolog," 78, and O'Laughlin, "The Bible, the Demons, and the Desert," 206–7.

[76] Coptic *Life of Evagrius* 17; trans. Vivian, *Four Desert Fathers*, 84–85.

modern readers can learn from it about several facets of early monastic life, as long as we keep in mind that the information it contains comes only from the monks around Evagrius and so cannot be taken as representative of all monks, not even all monks in Nitria and Kellia. Moreover, it is Evagrius who selected the data that appears here: he decided which features of monastic life to include, which to exclude, and whether and how to evaluate them negatively (as demonically inspired or exploited).[77]

The evidence of *Talking Back* suggests that many of the monks with whom Evagrius consulted came from relatively privileged social backgrounds. Monks remembered fondly the feasts that they used to enjoy in their pre-monastic lives (1.30, 36, 38–41), and they considered, sometimes with regret, the wealth and property that their families possessed (3.1, 3, 16–18, 22, 46, 50). Some monks remained entangled in worldly affairs through lawsuits (3.39), and others received criticism from friends and relatives when they failed to distribute their (presumably significant) wealth to them when they became monks (4.60). The prestige of a monk's relatives in the world could become a source of either discouragement (6.23) or pride (8.37). To be sure, Evagrius does mention monks whose families are poor (1.61) and monks who used to be or perhaps still are slaves (5.44). He speaks also of monks who are truly needy because, for example, illness has prevented them from working (3.7, 9, 10, 37, 38, 40, 57). But such poor monks usually appear as the potential objects of charity from the better-off monks whom Evagrius addresses. Monastic renunciation did not entirely erase the

---

[77] For more focused and detailed investigations of *Talking Back* (and other Evagrian works) along these lines, see David Brakke, "Making Public the Monastic Life: Reading the Self in Evagrius Ponticus' *Talking Back*," in *Religion and the Self in Antiquity*, ed. David Brakke, Michael L. Satlow, and Steven Weitzman, 222–33 (Bloomington: Indiana University Press, 2005), and David Brakke, "Care for the Poor, Fear of Poverty, and Love of Money: Evagrius Ponticus on the Monk's Economic Vulnerability," in *Wealth and Poverty in Early Church and Society*, ed. Susan Holman, 76–87 (Grand Rapids, MI.: Baker Academic, 2008). See also the earlier observations of O'Laughlin, "The Bible, the Demons, and the Desert," 207–11.

monks' differing social levels, as well-born monks looked down on their inferiors (8.37) or taunted former or current slaves (5.44).

The loosely knit ascetic community that these monks joined had its own economic life and measures of status. Most monks engaged in some form of manual labor, which could either become a source of dissatisfaction or be pursued too vigorously in pursuit of greater income (1.61, 63, 64; 3.29; 6.1, 28). It seems that some advanced monks told their disciples how much labor to perform, a custom that could leave the junior monk vulnerable to exploitation (3.4, 6, 8). Evagrius does not mention precisely what kind of work these monks did (other sources suggest that basket weaving was the archetypal monastic trade), but he does refer to trips to the market (2.58), to loans between monks (3.40), (possibly) to cattle that monks owned (5.18), and to cooperative ventures in which monks transacted business on behalf of the wider community or served as a "steward" or "overseer" (3.15, 56; 7.10). The necessities of life that the monk needed to acquire consisted primarily of such basics as food and clothing. The primary foodstuffs that Evagrius mentions are bread and oil (1.8); to abstain from oil was a severe ascetic discipline (1.18). Wine was available, although discouraged (1.22, 26, 35, 67); vegetables and fruits appear as special treats or temptations (1.32, 45, 53, 54). There are many references to possessions in general, but few to anything specific: Evagrius warns, for example, against using either refreshment for the brothers or acquisition of a Bible as the pretense for acquiring more things (3.35).

Like any collection of human beings, the early monastic community had its share of conflicts. Book 5 of *Talking Back*, on anger, concerns mostly the anger that monks felt toward one another. Monks gossiped maliciously about one another (5.4, 6, 11), accused one another of bad behavior (5.14), plotted against other monks (5.20), failed to repay loans (5.57), and held grudges (5.1). Monks complained that their leaders were uncaring, callous, or insufficiently experienced in the monastic life (6.2, 55; 8.8). Their peers too, they could say, were unfeeling (6.30) or such a bad influence that the better choice would be to live alone (7.11). In a community in which social rank was determined primarily by acknowledged wisdom, virtue, and success in the ascetic life, a certain amount of judging others and discussion of their virtues and shortcomings must have been necessary.[78] Without such discussions we would lack many of the *apophthegmata*. Yet such evaluation of self and others brought the monk into dangerous moral territory, which Evagrius considers here at length. To be sure, there were times when it was proper for one monk to chastise another (5.23). But especially for the advanced monk the danger of harshly or unfairly condemning other monks and believing oneself to be morally superior was very grave (8.31, 33, 38, 42, 49d, 53–54, 57).

If the moral scrutiny of his monastic brothers was not enough, the monk could also find himself the object of criticism or even persecution from his nonmonastic family members (5.34, 56), one sign of how the withdrawn monk remained connected to the world that he had left behind. Some monks wanted to try to persuade their skeptical relatives of the value of the monastic life, an impulse that Evagrius condemns as a desire to please people (7.39). Indeed, Evagrius shows no enthusiasm for the desire of monks to enter villages and cities even for seemingly good reasons, whether simply to teach (7.9, 18) or to encourage others to become monks (7.1). Monks could be indiscreet in talking to secular people about the monastic life (7.17). Still, there were several ways in which Evagrius's colleagues exercised authority in "the world": they settled disputes (7.12), served as guarantors for loans (7.16), and performed healings (7.35, 42). The wider church appears only occasionally in this work. It seems that monks were aware of the liturgical calendar and wanted to eat a little more on feast days (1.3, 29, 40, 60), which sometimes the leading monks allowed, to the mixed feelings of some (1.32). Ordination to the priesthood was the primary way that a monk might establish a formal connection to the church, and in *Talking Back*, as in Evagrius's other works, ordination consistently appears as a danger, fuel for the fire of pride (7.3, 8, 26, 36, 40).

---

[78] See Maud Gleason, "Visiting and News: Gossip and Reputation-Management in the Desert," *Journal of Early Christian Studies* 6 (1998): 501–21.

Finally, in these pages, we learn about some of the anxieties that troubled these monastic pioneers. Monks worried about the debilitating effects of their asceticism on their bodies (1.14, 19, 20, 43, 44, 47, 56, 57, 59, 65; 4.76) and about the health of their family members (4.42). They missed the relatives whom they had left (6.7, 43, 44, 53). They feared that they might go mad (4.43), and they fretted about the poor condition of their cells (6.26). They feared getting old (6.32). As we read about such touchingly human concerns, we cannot fail to feel somewhat closer to these ancient men who made the remarkable choice to seek God in the harsh desert. Yet the overall point of *Talking Back* is that these anxiety-producing obstacles to their knowledge of God were not natural human feelings to be understood, but suggestions of demons to be refuted. It is here that the spirituality of *Talking Back* becomes most distant from our ways of thinking about ourselves and so perhaps most able to say something new to us.

Note on Texts and Translations

Loukios's letter to Evagrius survives only in an Arabic version, published by Irénée Hausherr.[1] I made an initial draft translation from Hausherr's retroversion into Greek, and my colleague Professor Kevin Jaques compared this draft to the Arabic text and made suggestions for revision.

Evagrius's *Letter 4* survives completely only in a Syriac version, published by Wilhelm Frankenberg.[2] However, a Greek text for a substantial portion of the letter, running from the middle of section 3 to the end, appears in a thirteenth-century manuscript and has been published by Claire Guillaumont.[3] My translation follows the Syriac, but then switches to the Greek when it becomes extant. The section divisions follow those found in Gabriel Bunge's German translation.[4]

---

[1] Irénée Hausherr, "Eulogius—Loukios," *Orientalia Christiana Periodica* 6 (1940): 216–20.

[2] Wilhelm Frankenberg, *Euagrios Ponticus*, Abhandlungen der königlichen Gesellschaft der Wissenschaften zu Göttingen, Philologisch-historisch Klasse, Neue Folge 13.2 (Berlin: Weidmannsche Buchhandlung, 1912), 568.

[3] Claire Guillaumont, "Fragments grecs inédits d'Evagre le Pontique," in *Texte und Textkritik: Eine Aufsatzsammlung*, Texte und Untersuchungen zur Geschichte der altchristlichen Literatur 133, ed. Jürgen Dummer, 209–21 (Berlin: Akademie, 1987), at 219–20.

[4] Gabriel Bunge, *Evagrios Pontikos: Briefe aus der Wüste*, Sophia: Quellen östlicher Theologie 24 (Trier: Paulinus, 1986), 214–16.

The Greek text of *Talking Back* apparently does not survive. Complete versions are extant in Syriac and Armenian, and there are fragments in Georgian and Sogdian. I have not consulted the Armenian and Georgian texts at all.[5] In 1912 Frankenberg published the text of a single Syriac manuscript now in the British Library (B.L. Add. 14,578), which serves as the basis for this translation.[6] In the notes "MS" refers to B.L. Add. 14,578. In 1985 Nicholas Sims-Williams published an edition and translation of the Sogdian fragments.[7] The Sogdian fragments attest, although under a different numbering system, 1.3-10; 2.38-42, 46-50, 63-65; 3.2-7, 13, 17-19, 53-55, 58; 4.1-2, 35-36, 43-45: 6.20-24, 29-30.[8] As he edited the Sogdian fragments, Sims-Williams also collated B.L. Add. 14,578 and several other Syriac manuscripts against Frankenberg's text and noted several corrections and variants. I have sometimes incorporated these readings into my translation, especially when they agree with variants found in Sims-Williams's English translation of the Sogdian fragments, and I have noted these instances where they occur. In addition, I made my own collations from microfilms of the entire text of B.L. Add. 14,578 and of portions of the text found in B.L. Add. 12,175, which have resulted in a few more corrections to Frankenberg's text, also noted. I do not pretend to offer anything close to a new edition, which would require an account of all the surviving witnesses, including the Armenian and the Georgian. Should someone create such an edition, this translation would require replacement, but no one would be happier than I. I have benefited also from the several abridged or incomplete translations into modern languages that precede this one.

---

[5] Armenian: Barshegh Sargisean, *The Life and Works of the Holy Father Evagrius Ponticus in an Armenian Version of the Fifth Century with Introduction and Notes* (in Armenian) (Venice: S. Ghazar, 1907), 217–323.

[6] Frankenberg, *Euagrios*, 472–544.

[7] Nicholas Sims-Williams, *The Christian Sogdian Manuscript C2*, Schriften zur Geschichte und Kultur des alten Orients: Berliner Turfautexte 12 (Berlin: Akademie, 1985), 168–82.

[8] See the concordance at Sims-Williams, *Christian Sogdian Manuscript C2*, 181–82.

I have included all of the entries that appear in B.L. Add. 14,578, and I have followed its numbering system, with some corrections. The text in B.L. Add. 14,578 has 498 entries. Most modern scholars have counted 492 entries by adding the numbers that the manuscript gives for the final entries in each book. There is, however, one unnumbered entry in Book 4, following 4.19, and there are five in Book 8, following 8.49. These six unnumbered entries bring the total to 498. In the translation I have labeled these entries 4.19a and 4.19b, 8.49a, 8.49b, and so forth. It is likely that the scribe of the manuscript recalled the five unnumbered entries in Book 8, but not the one in Book 4, when he calculated a total of 497. There are also numbering problems in Book 3 at 3.19-27, which I have noted there and taken into account in my translation.

The only other Syriac manuscript that I have studied, B.L. Add. 12,175, contains fewer entries and uses a different numbering system. Like the Sogdian fragments, it numbers all the entries in the entire book sequentially and does not begin again with 1 at the beginning of each book. Thus, the first entry in Book 2 is numbered 70. The six unnumbered entries of 14,578 appear in this text in the same order and properly numbered, thus supporting their inclusion in this translation. The final entry in 12,175 is numbered 495, but this is a mistake: the text actually has 496 entries. 12,175 lacks two entries that appear in Book 3 in 14,578 (3.8, 10), and it contains numbering errors of its own. It uses each of the numbers 267 and 269 twice and does not use 419 at all, resulting in an undercount of 1. Although they share the same system, the numbering in the Sogdian fragments does not appear to match that of 12,175 precisely, suggesting either numbering errors or a different number of entries in that textual tradition. Any eventual critical edition of *Talking Back* will have to sort through such differences in numbering. It may be that the system in 12,175 and the Sogdian fragments is the more common one.

All that I have said thus far applies to the Syriac text of the prologue and the entries written by Evagrius. For the biblical passages I have translated the Greek text of either the Septuagint or the New Testament (with the exceptions of the two cases in which I have not identified the biblical passage), as have nearly all my modern predecessors as translators of this work. The Syriac text (at least that of B.L. Add. 14,578 and 12,175) is markedly influenced by the Peshitta, and in numerous cases the relevance of the biblical passage to the entry with which it is paired becomes clear only when one reads the Greek. To be sure, the texts of the modern editions of the Septuagint and the New Testament were not those known to Evagrius, but they are doubtless closer to what Evagrius read than what one finds in the Syriac manuscripts of *Talking Back*. I have not noted the numerous differences between the Syriac text of the biblical passages and the Greek, except in the few cases in which the differences are striking enough that one might question whether I have correctly identified the biblical passage that Evagrius meant. Neither have I noted instances in which Frankenberg's text of the Syriac must be corrected in the case of biblical passages. My references to Old Testament passages are to the Septuagint, even where the Syriac text uses a different reference (e.g., I cite as from 1 Kingdoms a passage that the Syriac text identifies as "from Samuel"). My translations from the New Testament are adapted from, but not always identical with, the New Revised Standard Version.

My citations of most other works of Evagrius follow Evagrius of Pontus, *The Greek Ascetic Corpus*, trans. Robert E. Sinkewicz, Oxford Early Christian Studies (Oxford: Oxford University Press, 2003).

Editorial Signs and Abbreviations

MS	B.L. Add. 14,578
12,175	B.L. Add. 12,175
< >	text restored by the translator, without attestation in any examined manuscript
[ ]	text added by the translator for clarity

Loukios, *Letter to Evagrius*

In the name of the Father and of the Son and of the Holy Spirit, a single God. Letter of the holy father Loukios to the holy father Evagrius. May God grant us the blessing of their prayers doubly.

You, O father, have lived in the desert, as if at a mother's breast, for these many years, doing battle with the invisible enemies. O honored father Evagrius, you have put on the weapons of the soul's fitting labors, and you have become such an experienced combatant against the spirits of wickedness that not only have you become an object of fear among the demons, but you have also summoned others, so that they too might become combatants against the evil spirits and filthy thoughts.

Therefore, I ask your fatherhood to classify the fight against the beings of darkness, and I entreat your holiness to compose for me some clear treatise concerning it and to acquaint me with the demons' entire treachery, which by their own efforts and according to their own undertaking they produce in the path of monasticism. Send it to us, so that we, your friends, might also easily cast off from ourselves those evil suggestions of theirs. For I know that you will attend to the one who requests from you spiritual things, and therefore I have addressed this to you. Farewell in the Lord.

Evagrius, *Letter* 4

1. I have seen the letter of your holiness, in which you amply demonstrated your love for us and commanded us to send you something from our labors. I had not wanted to send anything of my own accord because of my embarrassment in the face of your temperance. But now, because I have been commanded, I have readily obeyed and have sent you the treatise of responses, so that you might read it, correct it, and complete whatever is lacking, in case we have presented any of the unclean thoughts imprecisely or we have not properly found the answer that opposes them. I confess to your reverence that for some time I have not dealt with the demonic thoughts as one ought because I have been frequently hindered by them, and after your departure from me I have endured unspeakable sufferings from them. But now I praise our Lord because of the things that I have heard and learned about you, just as I have prayed.

2. Be for me, then, a proclaimer of continence, a listener of humility, and a destroyer "of thoughts and of every proud obstacle that is raised against the knowledge of Christ" [2 Cor 10:4–5], so that at the time of prayer the intellect might have the frankness of speech that belongs to those who transcend these [thoughts] and so that it [the intellect] might not be weighed or bent down because it is either knocked about by anger or drawn aside by desire. Such things happen to irascible and gluttonous persons who do not practice abstinence during the day and so do not escape evil illusions during the night.

3. So you too know through our Lord Jesus that reading the
divine Scriptures is very useful for purification because it removes
the intellect from this visible world's anxieties, from which stems
the perversity of unclean thoughts, which through their passions
bind the intellect and attach it to corporeal things. Do not hesitate,[1]
therefore, to converse with the brothers, to read the Scriptures at
the appointed time, not to "love the world and anything in the
world" [1 John 2:15], and to keep watch over thoughts, which is
a wolf-killing poison that the demons despise.

4. When the battle takes place with discernment, it is filled with
many thoughts, but it creates a great purity of thinking because
the demons can no longer mock or accuse the soul. For just as
practical wisdom is assigned the reasonable judgment of practical
matters, so too discernment is entrusted with the impressions that
occur in thinking, discerning holy and profane, clean and unclean
thoughts. And, according to the prophetic saying, it [discernment]
has experience of the tricks of the mocking demons, which imitate both perception and memory in order to deceive the rational
soul that strives for the knowledge of Christ.

5. And so everyone who has enlisted in this army must request
discernment from the Lord without neglecting the things that con-
tribute to the reception of this gift, which are, to speak in outline,
self-control, gentleness, keeping vigil, withdrawal, and frequent
prayers, which are supported by reading the divine Scriptures—for
nothing is as conducive to pure prayer as reading. Ascetic practice
cuts off the passions by destroying desire, sadness, and anger, but
the reading that follows it [ascetic practice] removes even love for
the representations by transferring it[2] to the formless, divine, and
simple knowledge, which the Lord symbolically named in the
gospels "room" [Matt 6:6], having indicated the hidden Father.

---

[1] Here begins the translation from the Greek fragment published by Claire
Guillaumont.

[2] Most likely "it" refers to the intellect, which does appear in the (otherwise
rather different) Syriac version.

Talking Back
A Treatise of Evagrius on the Eight Thoughts

PROLOGUE

[1] From the rational nature that is "beneath heaven" [Qo 1:13], part of it fights; part assists the one who fights; and part contends with the one who fights, strenuously rising up and making war against him. The fighters are human beings; those assisting them are God's angels; and their opponents are the foul demons. It is not because of the severity of the enemies' power, nor because of negligence on the part of the assistants, but because of slackening on the part of the fighters that knowledge of God disappears and perishes from them.

[2] Our Lord Jesus Christ, who gave up everything for our salvation, gave us the ability to "tread on snakes and scorpions, and over all the power of the enemy" [cf. Luke 10:19]. He handed on to us—along with the rest of all his teaching—what he himself did when he was tempted by Satan [Matt 4:1-11; Luke 4:1-13]. In the time of struggle, when the demons make war against us and hurl their arrows at us [cf. Eph 6:16], let us answer them from the Holy Scriptures, lest the unclean thoughts persist in us, enslave the soul through the sin of actual deeds, and so defile it and plunge it into the death brought by sin. For "the soul that sins shall die" [Ezek 18:4]. Whenever a thought is not firmly set in one's thinking, so that one can answer the evil one, sin is easily and swiftly

handled. This is wisely declared to us by Qoheleth, when he says, "No answer comes from those who perform evil quickly" [Qo 8:11]. Moreover, Solomon also says in his Proverbs, "Do not answer a fool in proportion to his folly, lest you become like him. Rather, answer a fool in opposition to his folly, lest he appear wise in his own eyes" [Prov 26:4-5].[1] That is, the person who commits an act of folly and becomes angry with his brother has answered, by his act, the fool "in proportion to his folly," and he has become like the demons,[2] for their anger is like "the raging serpent" [Deut 32:33]. But the person who is patient and says, "It is written, 'Cease from anger, and forsake wrath'" [Ps 36:8] has answered the fool "in opposition to his folly," and he has reproved the demon in its folly and showed it that he has learned that there is an antidote [against it] according to the Scriptures.

[3] Now, the words that are required for speaking against our enemies, that is, the cruel demons, cannot be found quickly in the hour of conflict, because they are scattered throughout the Scriptures and so are difficult to find. We have, therefore, carefully selected words from the Holy Scriptures, so that we may equip ourselves with them and drive out the Philistines forcefully, standing firm in the battle, as warriors and soldiers of our victorious King, Jesus Christ.

[4] Let us understand this, my beloved: to the extent that we resist the demons in the conflict and answer them with a word, they will become all the more embittered against us. This we learn from Job when he said, "Whenever I begin to speak, they wound me" [Job 6:4], and also from David when he said, "I am peaceful. Whenever I spoke to them, they made war against me gratuitously" [Ps 119:7]. But we must not be shaken by them; rather, we must resist them by relying on the power of our Savior. For if we place

---

[1] MS: "Rather, answer a fool according to your wisdom . . ." The LXX passage distinguishes between answering a fool "in proportion to" (*pros*) his folly and answering a fool "in opposition to" (*kata*) his folly, and it is this distinction that Evagrius seeks to clarify. The Syriac translator perhaps misunderstood the particular meaning of *kata* here and so falsely corrected the text.

[2] 12,175 reads the singular "demon."

our trust in Christ and keep his commandments, we will cross over the Jordan and capture the city of palms.[3] In this battle we need weapons of the spirit [cf. Eph 6:11-13], which are the true faith and, second, the teaching, which is a perfect fast, hard-won victories, humility, stillness—to be moved only barely or not to be moved at all—and unceasing prayer [cf. 1 Thess 5:17]. I would be amazed if there were a person who could fight the battle that takes place in the intellect or could be crowned with the garlands of righteousness [cf. 2 Tim 4:7-8] while satisfying himself with bread and water, something that quickly stirs up his anger and causes him to despise and neglect prayer and to associate with heretics. For St. Paul said, "Athletes exercise self-control in all things" [1 Cor 9:25] and to all people they show constant humility [cf. Titus 3:2], lifting up their hands everywhere without anger or evil intentions [cf. 1 Tim 2:8].

[5] Therefore, it is proper for us, when we labor at this task, to equip ourselves with the weapons of the spirit [cf. Eph 6:11-13] and to show the Philistines that we will fight against sin to the point of blood [cf. Heb 12:4], as we destroy evil intentions and "every proud obstacle raised up against the knowledge of God" [2 Cor 10:5]. We are zealous, so that "we will stand before the judgment seat of Christ" [Rom 4:10; 2 Cor 5:10] not merely as a monastic man but as a monastic intellect. For a monastic man is one who has departed from the sin that consists of deeds and action, while a monastic intellect is one who has departed from the sin that arises from the thoughts that are in our intellect and who at the time of prayer sees the light of the Holy Trinity.[4]

[6] Now, however, is the time, "through the power of our Lord Jesus Christ" [1 Cor 5:4] to contend first with the thoughts of the demon of gluttony and, after these, with the thoughts of the seven

---

[3] That is, Jericho (Deut 34:3); see *Thoughts* 20. Here the Jordan River represents the border between the "desert" of ascetic practice (*praktikē*) and the "promised land" of knowledge (*theoretikē*) (Gabriel Bunge, "Evagrios Pontikos: Der Prolog des 'Antirrhetikos,'" *Studia Monastica* 39 [1997]: 76–105, at 91, citing *Kephalaia Gnostica* 6.49 and *Scholia on Proverbs* 17.2).

[4] See *Reflections* 15–16.

other demons, which I have written in sequence at the beginning of the book on the monastic life.[5] I have struggled "to open my mouth" [Ps 118:131] and to speak to God, to his holy angels, and to my own afflicted soul. I have made public the entire contest of the monastic life, which the Holy Spirit taught David through the Psalms and the blessed fathers handed over to us, but which I have named in this book after these [demons]. For us the entire struggle will take place through the thoughts that approach us from each of these eight demons. But I have written and quoted for each of the thoughts an answer from the Holy Scriptures that is able to cut it off.

---

[5] Evagrius refers to the *Praktikos*, in which he lists the eight thoughts or demons in chapter 6: see the discussion of Antoine Guillaumont and Claire Guillaumont in Evagrius Ponticus, *Traité pratique, ou Le moine*, Sources chrétiennes 170–71 (Paris: Éditions du Cerf, 1971) 1:405–6.

FIRST BOOK

Against the Thoughts of Gluttony

From the Book of Genesis

1. Against the thoughts that seek without the labor of fasting to cultivate the rational land:

   Issachar has desired that which is good, resting between the inheritances. And because he saw that the resting place is good and the land is fertile, he subjected his shoulder to labor and became a farmer (Gen 49:14–15).

From Exodus

2. Against the thought that says to me, "Do not torment your soul with a lot of fasting that gains you nothing and does not purify your intellect":

   He made the bronze basin and its bronze stand from the mirrors of the women who fasted, who fasted by the doors of the tabernacle of witness, in the day in which he set it up (Exod 38:26).[1]

---

[1] MS: "He made the bronze basin and its bronze stand for the washing of the women who fasted and came to pray at the door of the tabernacle" (cf. Exod 30:18, from which likely comes the phrase "for the washing"). The entry number "2" is missing in the MS, but appears in 12,175.

\<From Numbers\>

3. Against the thoughts that stir up in us the desire to eat meat on a feast day and that advise us also to eat on account of the body's illness:

> And to the people say, "Purify yourselves for tomorrow, and you shall eat meat. . . . You shall not eat one day, not two, not five days, not ten days, and not twenty days. For a month of days you shall eat, until it [the meat] comes out of your nostrils. And it shall be nausea to you because you disobeyed the Lord, who is among you" (Num 11:18-20).

From Deuteronomy

4. Against the thought that seeks to be filled with food and drink and gives no heed to the harm that springs from filling the belly:

> Having eaten and been filled, pay attention to yourself, lest you forget the Lord your God, who brought you out of the land of Egypt, out of the house of slavery (Deut 6:11-12).[2]

5. Against the thought that says to me, "The command to fast is burdensome":[3]

> The command that I give you this day is not burdensome, nor is it far from you (Deut 30:11).

6. Against the thought that desires to be filled[4] with food and drink and supposes that nothing evil for the soul comes from them:

> And Jacob ate and was filled, and the beloved one kicked; he grew fat and became thick and broad, and he abandoned the God who made him and departed from God his Savior (Deut 32:15).

---

[2] The entry number "4" is missing in the MS, but appears in 12,175.

[3] Frankenberg's text incorrectly lacks a daleth before *yqyr*.

[4] Frankenberg's text incorrectly gives *dtsbl*, while the MS has *dtsbᶜ*.

From Samuel

7. Against the thought of gluttony that compels me to eat at the ninth hour:

> God do so to me and more besides if I eat bread or anything else before the sun goes down (2 Kgdms 3:35).

From the Book of Kings

8. Against the thought that suggests to me the loss of bread, oil, and other things that we need:

> Thus says the Lord, "The jar of meal will not run out, and the jug of oil will not be diminished, until the day when the Lord gives rain upon the earth" (3 Kgdms 17:14).

9. Against the soul that wants to follow the path of the saints while being full of bread and water:

> And the king of Israel said, "Take Michaias and send him to Semer the ruler of the city, and tell Joas the ruler's son to put him in prison and to have him eat bread of affliction and water of affliction until I return in peace" (3 Kgdms 22:26-27).

10. Against the thought that says to us, "Look, the provisions that we have gathered are not sufficient both for us and for the brothers who come to us":

> For thus says the Lord, "They will eat and leave [some remaining]." And they ate and left [some remaining], according to the word of the Lord (4 Kgdms 4:43-44).

From David

11. Against the thought that embitters me in the life of harsh poverty:

> The Lord shepherds me, and I will lack nothing (Ps 22:1).

12. Against the thought that, even when there is no scarcity, gathers more bread than it needs, on the pretext of hospitality:

> I was young, and I have indeed grown old. I have not seen a righteous person abandoned or his progeny seeking bread (Ps 36:25).

13. Against the thought that is attentive to food and clothing, but rejects attention to the truth:

> I will declare my iniquity and I will attend to my sin (Ps 37:19).

14. Against the thoughts that advise us and say, "Do not live so severely; through fasting and constant labor you will wear out your weak body":

> And he labored forever, and he will live to the end, so that he will not see corruption when he sees sages dying (Ps 48:10).[5]

15. Against the thought that says to me, "Do not wear yourself out so unsparingly and afflict your soul by keeping vigil":

> A broken and contrite heart God will not despise (Ps 50:19).

16. Against the thought that is anxious about food and drink and diligent about where it can get them:

> Cast your anxiety upon the Lord, and he will sustain you (Ps 54:23).[6]

17. Against the thought that suggests to me, "Keeping vigil does not benefit you at all; rather, it gathers many thoughts against you":

> I have watched and have become like a sparrow dwelling alone on a roof (Ps 101:8).[7]

---

[5] The entry number "14" is missing in the MS, but appears in 12,175.

[6] Evagrius often cites this verse in urging the monk to overcome anxiety about having enough: see *Foundations of the Monastic Life* 4; *To Eulogios* 28.30; *Thoughts* 6.

[7] Evagrius calls the vigilant monk a sparrow in *To Monks* 46.

18. Against the thought that rebukes us because we abstain from oil and that does not remember that David did this and said:

> My knees have become weak from fasting, and my flesh has been altered by [the lack of] oil (Ps 108:24).

19. Against the thoughts that hinder us from our way of life by instilling fear in us and saying, "A miserable death results from austere fasting":

> I will not die, but live, and I will recount the Lord's works (Ps 117:17).

20. Against the thoughts that persuade me to desist a little from keeping frequent vigils and to give a little rest to the weak and miserable body:

> I will not go into the tabernacle of my house; I will not get up upon the couch of my bed; I will not give sleep to my eyes nor drowsiness to my eyelids nor rest to my temples, until I find a place for the Lord, a tabernacle for the God of Jacob (Ps 131:3-5).

From the Proverbs of Solomon

21. Against the thought that predicts to us that famine or great affliction is coming soon:

> The Lord will not famish a righteous soul, but he will overthrow the life of the ungodly (Prov 10:3).

22. Against the thought that suggests to me desire for wine on the pretext that the liver and spleen are harmed by water:

> He who takes pleasure in banquets of wine will leave dishonor in his strongholds (Prov 12:11a).

23. Against the thought that is bound by concern about the desire for foods and rejects concern about achievements in virtue:

> With everyone who is careful there is abundance, but the pleasure-taking and the indolent will be in want (Prov 14:23).

24. Against the thought that weeps over simple foods and dry bread:

> A morsel with pleasure in peace is better than a house full of many good things and unjust sacrifices with strife (Prov 17:1).

25. Against the thoughts that persuade us on a feast day to show a little mercy to our body by offering it a few delicacies:

> Delight does not suit a fool, [nor is it proper] if a servant begins to rule with arrogance (Prov 19:10).

26. Against the thought that, in the absence of serious illness, coaxes us to drink wine and prophesies to us about pain in the stomach and the entire digestive system:

> Wine is an intemperate thing, and drunkenness leads to insolence, and anyone who is tangled up in it is no sage (Prov 20:1).

27. Against the thought that seizes our intellect so that we bind ourselves to our fast and our ascetic practice by our oaths, something that is foreign to the monastic way of life:

> It is a trap for a man hastily to consecrate some of his possessions, for regret comes after the making of the vow (Prov 20:25).

28. Against the thought that hinders us by suggesting that we not give from our bread to those in need and by saying to me, "That person can [find mercy] anywhere, but we cannot approach any stranger's door":

> The one who shows mercy will himself be supported, for he gave to the poor from his own bread (Prov 22:9).

29. Against the thoughts that on a feast day gently approach us and say to us that we might just once in a long stretch of time taste meat and wine:

> Do not be a wine-drinker, and do not stay long at feasts and sales of meat, for every drunkard and customer of prostitutes will be poor, and every sluggard will clothe himself in tattered and ragged garments (Prov 23:20-21).

1. *Against the Thoughts of Gluttony*

30. Against the thought that recalls delicacies of the past and remembers pleasant wines and the cups that we used to hold in our hands when we would recline at table and drink:

> For if you set your eyes on bowls and cups, you later will go more naked than a pestle. At the end he stretches himself out like someone struck by a snake and through whom venom is diffused as by a horned serpent (Prov 23:31-32).

31. Against the thoughts that entice us to fill our belly with bread and water:

> Do not give the bed of a righteous man to a sinner, and do not go astray in satiety of the couch.[8]

32. Against the thoughts that we have in opposition to the shame in which we respect the fathers when they persuade us to relax the fast and to eat vegetables during a feast:

> For there is a shame that brings sin, and a shame that is glory and grace (Sir 4:21).

33. Against the demon that persuades me through its flattery and says to me with promises, "You will no longer suffer any harm from food and drink because your body is weak and dry from prolonged fasting":

> A weeping enemy promises everything with his lips, but in his heart he contrives deceits (Prov 26:24).

34. Against the thought that shows me God's commandments as if they were difficult and tells me that they bring many difficulties and miseries upon the body and soul:

> The wounds of a friend are more trustworthy than the spontaneous kisses of an enemy (Prov 27:6).

---

[8] The text for nos. 31–32 may be corrupt. The biblical quotation for no. 31 is not clear. 12,175 reads "satiety of the belly" rather than "satiety of the couch." Number 32 possibly contains remnants of two entries ("against the thought that . . ."; "against the shame that . . ."), and its quotation comes from Sirach, not Proverbs.

From Qoheleth[9]

35. Against the thought that asks for a little wine in the absence of illness and says to me, "Look, it was for the sake of human beings that wine was created":

    He has made all things beautiful in his season (Qo 3:11).

36. Against the thought that reminds me of past feasting and drinking and wants [to return to] this custom:

    It is better to go into a house of mourning than to go into a house of drinking (Qo 7:2).

37. Against the vain thought that persuades us to extend our discipline beyond what is appropriate by putting sackcloth on our loins, setting out for the desert, living continuously under the sky, and tending wild plants; and that advises us as well to flee from the sight of human beings who comfort us and who are comforted by us:

    Do not be very righteous or especially wise, lest you be deceived (Qo 7:16).

From Job

38. Against the thoughts that remind us of past feasts and show us the difficulty that has occurred:

    If we have received good things from the Lord's hand, shall we not endure evil things? (Job 2:10).

From Micah[10]

39. Against the soul's thought that travels to its corporeal kinfolk and finds a table filled with all kinds of foods:

    Get up and leave, for this is not your place of rest because of uncleanness (Mic 2:10).

---

[9] This heading is missing in the MS, but appears in 12,175.

[10] This heading is missing in the MS, but appears in 12,175.

From Habakkuk

40. Against the thought of gluttony that on feast days enumerates for me many people reclining at the finest table, exulting and rejoicing:[11]

> But I will exult in the Lord and rejoice in God my Savior (Hab 3:18).

From Isaiah

41. Against the thoughts that remind us of pleasures and of a table that has been filled with all good things and praise these things as better than the monastic life:[12]

> Woe to those who call evil good and good evil, who make darkness light and light darkness, who make bitter sweet and sweet bitter (Isa 5:20).

42. Against the soul's thought that has become tired and weary of the hunger that comes with little bread and scant water:

> And the Lord will give you bread of affliction and scant water, and yet those who deceive you will no longer come near you; for your eyes will see those who deceive you, and your ears will hear the words of those who went after you to lead you astray (Isa 30:20-21).

From Jeremiah

43. To the Lord concerning the infirmity of my body, which has been weakened by much fasting and diminished by an austere

---

[11] MS: "Against the thought of gluttony that on feast days shows us many people reclining at table < . . .>, exulting and rejoicing." 12,175 reads "enumerates for me" and fills the lacuna.

[12] MS: "Against the thoughts that remind us of the pleasures of a table that has been filled with good < . . . > and praise them as better than the monastic life." The translation reflects the text of 12,175.

discipline, and concerning my soul, which is filled with evil thoughts of fornication:

> Lord, remember me and visit me, and vindicate me from before those who persecute me without delay. Know how I have received reproach for your sake from those who set at naught your words (Jer 15:15).

44. To the Lord concerning the demon that chills the stomach and all the sinews of the body, and casts great weakness into the body as if from hunger and prolonged illness:

> See, Lord, that I am afflicted, that my belly is troubled and my heart is turned within me (Lam 1:20).

From Daniel[13]

45. Against the soul that is not satisfied with bread for food and water for drink, but wants vegetables along with these, and does not remember the affliction of the seeds that Daniel and his companions ate:

> Then Daniel said to Amelsad, whom the chief eunuch had set over Daniel, Hananiah, Mishael, and Azariah, "Test your children for ten days, and give us seeds, and let us eat, and let us drink water. And let our appearance be seen by you and the appearance of the children that eat at the king's table, and deal with your servants as you see." And he listened to them and tested them for ten days. And at the end of the ten days, their appearance looked better and stronger in flesh than the children who ate at the king's table. And Amelsad took away their supper and the wine of their drink, and he gave them seeds (Dan 1:11–16).[14]

---

[13] The MS lacks "Daniel," which appears in 12,175.

[14] Ironically, in *Thoughts* 35 Evagrius says that the demon of gluttony may adduce this story about Daniel and his companions in order to tempt the monk to undertake too severe an ascetic regime with respect to food.

From the Gospel of Matthew

46. Against the soul that at the time of attack wants to find strong armor:

> Then Jesus was led up by the Spirit into the wilderness to be tempted by the devil. He fasted forty days and forty nights, and afterwards he was famished (Matt 4:1-2).

47. Against the thoughts that are anxious about food and clothing on the pretexts of hospitality, illnesses, and prolonged miseries of the body:

> Do not worry about your life, what you will eat or what you will drink, or about your body, what you will wear. Is not life more than food, and the body more than clothing? (Matt 6:25).[15]

48. Against the soul that is bound by gluttony and supposes that by refreshing the body with delicacies it travels the road of life:

> For the gate is narrow and the road is hard that leads to life, and there are few who take it (Matt 7:14).

From the Gospel of Luke

49. Against the thought that hinders us from giving to the needy from our food and clothing on the pretexts, "The provisions are not enough for both us and them" or "There is someone weaker or in greater need than this person, and we should give to that person rather than this one, for this one is lazy and wants to eat and be clothed without working":

> Whoever has two coats must share with anyone who has none; and whoever has food must do likewise (Luke 3:11).

---

[15] See *Thoughts* 6 for a discussion of freedom from anxiety that also cites this verse.

From Acts

50. Against the soul that loves the desires and collects food and clothing for itself alone:

   All who believed were together and had all things in common; they would sell their possessions and goods and distribute the proceeds to all, as any had need (Acts 2:44–45).[16]

51. Against the soul that grows weary in the affliction that comes upon it from restriction of bread and water:

   It is through many afflictions that we must enter the kingdom of God (Acts 14:22).

The Apostle: From the Letter to the Romans

52. Against the thoughts that persuade us to show a little care for our body by eating and drinking:

   Make no provision for the flesh, to gratify its desires (Rom 13:14).

53. Against the thoughts that entice us to be comforted with a little treat of vegetables:

   The weak eat vegetables (Rom 14:2).

From the First Letter to the Corinthians

54. Against the thought that at harvest time casts into us the desire for fruits:

   Athletes exercise self-control in all things; they do it to receive a perishable wreath, but we an imperishable one (1 Cor 9:25).

---

[16] The entry number "50" is missing in the MS, but appears in 12,175.

From the Second Letter to the Corinthians

55. Against the thoughts that arise in us because of great need and that gradually relax the soul's vigor:

> We are afflicted in every way, but not crushed; perplexed, but not driven to despair; persecuted, but not forsaken; struck down, but not destroyed; always carrying in the body the death of Jesus, so that the life of Jesus may also be made visible in our bodies (2 Cor 4:8–10).

56. Against the thought that depicts before our eyes a disease of the stomach, liver, and spleen, and a blowing that exceeds [the capacity of] the navel:

> So we do not lose heart. Even though our outer nature is wasting away, our inner nature is being renewed day by day (2 Cor 4:16).

57. Against the thoughts that arise in us as our entire body becomes gradually corrupted:

> For we know that if the earthly tent we live in is destroyed, we have a building from God, a house not made with hands, eternal in the heavens (2 Cor 5:1).

58. Against the thought that arouses compassion in us, persuades us to give to the poor, and afterward makes us sad and annoyed about what we gave:

> Not reluctantly or under compulsion, for God loves a cheerful giver, and the one who has compassion on the poor will be supported (2 Cor 9:7; Prov 22:8–9).[17]

59. Against the thought that depicts in us severe weakness from diseases that are about to arise in us from fasting, and that persuades us to eat a little cooked food:

> For whenever I am weak, then I am strong (2 Cor 12:10).

---

[17] The MS has combined the two passages.

From the Letter to the Ephesians[18]

60. Against the thought that wants to be filled with wine on a feast day:

> Do not get drunk with wine, for that is debauchery; but be filled with the Spirit, as you sing psalms and hymns and spiritual songs among yourselves, singing and making melody to the Lord in your hearts (Eph 5:18-19).[19]

From the Letter to the Philippians

61. Against the thoughts that make our soul neither want to gather provisions through manual labor nor be persuaded to receive something from its family because they are poor and reside at a great distance, but rather advise it to fill its need from others:

> The Lord is near. Do not worry about anything, but in everything by prayer and supplication with thanksgiving let your requests be made known to God (Phil 4:5-6).

62. Against the thought that predicts to me hunger and loss of bread and suggests to me the disgrace of receiving a favor from others:

> In any and all circumstances I have learned the secret of being well fed and of going hungry, of having plenty and of being in need. I can do all things through him who strengthens me (Phil 4:12-13).[20]

---

[18] "From" is missing in the MS, but appears in 12,175.

[19] The number "60" is missing in the MS, but appears in 12,175.

[20] Evagrius warns elsewhere against feeling ashamed to accept material help from others: *Foundations of the Monastic Life* 4; *Praktikos* 9.

From the First Letter to the Thessalonians

63. Against the thought that hinders us from working with our hands and persuades us to expect to receive what we need from others:

> But we urge you, brothers, to do so more and more, to aspire to live quietly, to mind your own affairs, and to work with your hands, as we directed you, so that you may behave properly toward outsiders and be dependent on no one (1 Thess 4:10–12).

From the Second Letter to the Thessalonians

64. Against the thinking that hinders us from working with our hands and compels us to eat bread and to fill ourselves:

> Anyone unwilling to work should not eat (2 Thess 3:10).

From the Letter to the Hebrews

65. Against the thought that says that the monastic discipline is difficult and extremely burdensome, that through affliction it cruelly lays waste to our body, and that it does not profit the soul:

> Now, discipline always seems painful rather than pleasant at the time, but later it yields the peaceful fruit of righteousness to those who have been trained by it (Heb 12:11).

66. Against the thinking that is diligent about food and neglects compassion for the needy:

> Do not neglect to do good and to share what you have, for such sacrifices are pleasing to God (Heb 13:16).

From the First Letter to Timothy

67. Against the thought that, in the absence of pain in the stomach and severe illnesses, advises us to drink wine by suggesting to us the blessed Apostle's direction when in his letter he commanded Timothy on this point:

> **Keep yourself pure. No longer drink only water, but take a little wine for the sake of your stomach and your frequent ailments** (1 Tim 5:22-23).

From the Letter of James

68. Against the thoughts that turn us back toward the world and its commandments:

> **Do you not know that friendship with the world is enmity with God? Therefore, whoever wishes to be a friend of the world becomes an enemy of God** (Jas 4:4).

From the Letter of John

69. Against the thought that supposes that the commandment to fast is burdensome:

> **And his commandments are not burdensome, for whatever is born of God conquers the world. And this is the victory that conquers the world, our faith** (1 John 5:3-4).

Blessed is our Lord Jesus Christ, our God, who has given us the victory over the thoughts of the demon of gluttony!

SECOND BOOK

Against the Thoughts of Fornication

From Exodus

1. Against the thought of fornication that depicts in my intellect a married woman:

   You shall not covet your neighbor's wife (Exod 20:17).[1]

2. Against the thought of sadness that arises in us due to the many temptations of fornication that come upon us and cut off our hope by saying to us, "What beautiful thing do you expect after all this labor?":

   If you indeed listen to my voice and do all the things that I will say to you, I will be an enemy to your enemies and an adversary to your adversaries. For my angel will go as your leader and will bring you to the Amorite, and Hittite, and Perizzite, and Canaanite, and Gergesite, and Hivite, and Jebusite, and I will destroy them (Exod 23:22-23).

3. Against the thought that supposes that in a single hour the evil thoughts of fornication will flee from it:

   I will not cast them out in one year, lest the land become desolate and the beasts of the land multiply against you. Gradually I will cast them out from before you, until you have increased and will inherit the land (Exod 23:29-30).

---

[1] The entries in this book are numbered 70 through 134 in 12,175.

4. Against the thought that comes from fornication and says, "Youth can never cease from the desires of fornication and offer to God thoughts purified of it":

> Everyone who is registered from age twenty and older shall offer the sacrifice to the Lord (Exod 30:14).

5. Against the thought of fornication that says, "Youth is neither guilty nor culpable if it fornicates or if it gladly receives unclean thoughts":

> And the Lord said to Moses, "If anyone has sinned against me, I will wipe them out of my book" (Exod 32:33).

From Deuteronomy

6. Against the intellect that does not make a vigilant effort to preserve itself from the fornication that is established within it, but rather speaks and performs wickedness with a woman that is depicted before its eyes:

> And hear, Israel, and observe so as to do them, so that it may be well with you and so that you may be greatly multiplied, just as the Lord God of your fathers said that he would give you a land flowing with milk and honey (Deut 6:3).

<7.> Against the thought that seeks, through filthy desire, to approach the demon of fornication:

> You shall fear the Lord your God, and serve only him, and cleave to him, and swear by his name (Deut 6:13).

8. Against the soul that day and night is harassed by thoughts of fornication, losing hope that it will gain victory over them:

> But if you should say in your thinking, "This nation is greater than I: how will I be able to destroy them?" you shall not fear them. Remember what the Lord your God did to Pharaoh and all the Egyptians (Deut 7:17-18).

9. Against the thought of the soul that is oppressed by thoughts of fornication, which divide the evil passion of fornication into diverse images, collect impure thoughts, put them in rotation, [then] cleave to one of these enslaving thoughts and make it persist upon the weak soul:

> And you will know today that the Lord your God will advance before you. He is a consuming fire. He will destroy them and turn them back from before you, and he will destroy them quickly, just as the Lord said to you (Deut 9:3).

10. Against the thoughts that turn quickly to foods whenever the spirit of fornication, playing with them, gives them a little respite and so they suppose that they have reached the frontier of chastity:

> You shall not do all that we do here today, each person [doing] what is pleasing to him. For up to now you have not reached the rest and inheritance that the Lord your God gives you (Deut 12:8-9).

11. Against the soul that is frightened and shaken by the demon that touches its members; those who have been tempted by this demon consider what has been said:

> Your helper will hold his shield over you, and his sword is your boast; and your enemies will lie to you, and you will tread upon their neck (Deut 33:29).

From Judges

12. Against the soul that due to sadness falls into listlessness and so is no longer able to endure the filthy thoughts that defile its prayer:

> Rise up, for this is the day on which the Lord has delivered Sisera into your hand; for the Lord will advance before you (Judg 4:14).

13. Against the intellect that is contending with thoughts of fornication, but does not want to shake them off of it completely and does not recognize the fetter of sin and the anxiety of evils:

> And Delilah said, "The Philistines are upon you, Samson!" And he woke up from his sleep and said, "I will go out just like every other time, and I will shake them off." And he did not know that the Lord had departed from him. And the Philistines seized him, cut out his eyes, brought him down to Gaza, and bound him with fetters of brass; and he ground at the mill in the prison house (Judg 16:20–21).

From Samuel

14. To the angel of the Lord that suddenly appeared in my intellect, cooled the thought of fornication, and drove out from it [my intellect] all the thoughts that besieged it:

> My heart is established in the Lord; my horn is exalted in my God; my mouth is enlarged over my enemies; I have rejoiced in your salvation (1 Kgdms 2:1).

15. Against the filthy demon of fornication that appeared to me at night in an obscene vision in the form of a woman, but which could not compel my soul with its filthy desires:

> The bow of the mighty ones has become weak, and the weak ones have girded themselves with strength. Those who were full of bread have been brought low, and the hungry have forsaken the land (1 Kgdms 2:4–5).

16. Against the soul that does not want to escape unclean desire but persists in the thought of Nahash the Ammonite, which [Nahash] is translated "snake":

> And all the men of Jabesh said to Nahash the Ammonite, "Make a covenant with us, and we will serve you." And Nahash the Ammonite said to them, "On these terms I will make a covenant with you, that I should put out all your right eyes and I will lay a reproach upon Israel" (1 Kgdms 11:1–2).

From the Book of Kings

17. Against the demon of fornication that wants to spoil and defile my chastity through thoughts:

> My God forbid that I should give you the inheritance of my fathers (3 Kgdms 20:3).

From the Book of Chronicles

18. Against the soul that supposes that it is tempted by the demon of fornication beyond its power:

> Then the land began to be subject to tribute to give silver at the command of Pharaoh, and each person according to his ability paid the silver and gold required by the people of the land to give to Pharaoh Neco (2 Chr 36:4a).

From Ezra [2]

19. To the Lord concerning the thoughts of fornication that show us abominable visions at night:

> And I said, "Lord, I am too ashamed and confounded, my God, to lift my face to you, for our transgressions have multiplied upon our head, and our trespasses have increased even to heaven. From the days of our fathers we have been in a trespass until this day" (2 Esd 9:6-7).

20. Against the soul that after valiant combats with thoughts of fornication has acquired chastity and purity:

> The land into that you enter to inherit is disturbed by the removal of the peoples of the nations for their abominations, with which they filled it from mouth to mouth with their acts of uncleanness (2 Esd 9:11).

---

[2] This heading actually appears before no. 20. It appears in this incorrect place in 12,175 as well.

From David the Prophet

21. To the Lord concerning the multitude of unclean thoughts
    that trouble and afflict us and attract our intellect to diverse
    faces:

    > Lord, why are they who afflict me so numerous? Many rise up
    > against me. Many say to my soul, "There is no salvation for
    > him in his God." But you, Lord, are my helper, my glory, and
    > the one who lifts up my head (Ps 3:2-4).

22. Against the soul that does not know that the intensity of
    irascibility opposes the thought of fornication, because iras-
    cibility comes from fire by nature, but unclean thoughts are
    born of water:

    > Be angry, and do not sin. Speak in your hearts, and feel com-
    > punction upon your beds (Ps 4:5; cf. Eph 4:26).[3]

23. Against the unclean thoughts that persist in us and frequently
    depict in us obscene images and that bind our intellect with
    passions of desire in our dishonorable members:

    > Depart from me, all your workers of iniquity, for the Lord has
    > heard the sound of my weeping; the Lord has heard my peti-
    > tion; the Lord has accepted my prayer (Ps 6:9-10).

24. To the Lord concerning the demon of fornication that, when
    it cannot humiliate us through the desire of our body, then
    shows us in our intellect a monk performing the obscene sin
    of fornication:

    > The swords of the enemy have failed utterly, and you have
    > destroyed cities. Their memory has been destroyed with a
    > noise, but the Lord endures forever (Ps 9:7-8).

25. To the Lord concerning the filthy demon of fornication that
    openly approaches the thighs of those who endeavor to de-
    part from it, suddenly seizing the intellect with a madness

---

[3] On the use of irascibility to oppose thoughts of fornication, see *Thoughts* 16,
also citing Ps 4:5.

that alters the soul through a multitude of powerful thoughts of fornication—it is very useful when we are tempted by this demon to jump up at once and to use our cell for frequent and brisk walks—let the one who is able to understand, understand:

> Light up my eyes, lest I sleep unto death, lest at any time my enemy say, "I have prevailed against him" (Ps 12:4-5).[4]

26. Against the soul that supposes that the thoughts of fornication are more powerful than God's commandments, which were given to us for the extirpation of this passion:

> I will beat them like the dust before the wind, and I will grind them like the mud of the streets (Ps 17:43).

27. To the Lord concerning the demon that suddenly fell upon the body, but could not conquer the intellect through the unclean thoughts that attacked it:

> You have turned my sorrow into dance for me; you have ripped off my sackcloth and have girded me with gladness, so that my glory may sing praise to you and I may not be pierced (Ps 29:12-13).

28. Against the thought that says to me, "The demon of fornication will put you to shame if you stand up to it in battle":

> Let those who seek my soul be put to shame and confounded; let those who devise evils against me be turned back and put to shame (Ps 34:4).

29. Against the thought that threatens me, "Another demon of fornication—weightier, bolder, and stronger than the first—is being sent to you, one that will easily compel your soul and bring it to the sin that is accomplished in deeds":

> Let them be as dust before the wind, with an angel of the Lord afflicting them. Let their way be dark and slippery, with an angel of the Lord persecuting them (Ps 34:5-6).

---

[4] Evagrius attributes this boast to the demon of listlessness in *Thoughts* 35.

30. Against the soul that, when it is being harassed by thoughts of fornication, rejects sackcloth and does not remember that David did this very thing for our instruction when he said:

> **But as for me, when they troubled me, I put on sackcloth and humbled my soul with fasting** (Ps 34:13).

31. Against the soul that is saddened because the filthy thoughts of fornication have persisted in it and that does not expect victory over them because it sees that one of the filthy images is fixed in its intellect and continually harasses it:

> **Yet a little while, and the sinner will not exist, and you will seek his place, and you will not find it** (Ps 36:10).

32. Against the demon of fornication that imitates the form of a beautiful naked woman, luxurious in her gait, her entire body obscenely dissipated, [a woman] who seizes the intellect of many persons and makes them forget the better things:

> **Therefore, may God destroy you forever; may he pluck you up and remove you from your dwelling and your root from the land of the living** (Ps 51:7).

33. Against the thought that prophesies to me that I will fall away from chastity and be put to shame before human beings:

> **Let all who hate Zion be put to shame and turned back. Let them be like the grass of the housetops, which withers before it is plucked up** (Ps 128:5-6).

From the Proverbs of Solomon

34. Against the demon of fornication that in a dream at night drew me into filthy behavior and then during the day through thoughts taunted us and laughed at us:

> **Therefore, I too will laugh at your destruction, and I will rejoice over you when ruin comes upon you, and when fear suddenly comes upon you and your overthrow comes like a tempest** (Prov 1:26-27).

35. Against the thoughts that compel us to linger in conversation with a married woman on the pretext that she has visited us frequently or that she will benefit spiritually from us:

> Do not be long with someone else's woman (Prov 5:20).

36. Against the intellect in which is depicted the form of a beautiful woman and that wants to speak with her earnestly or to do something evil that would not be proper, as the holy John, the prophet of Thebes,[5] recounted to us:

> Let not the desire for beauty conquer you; do not be ensnared by your eyes nor captured by her eyelids. For the price of a harlot is as much as one loaf of bread (Prov 6:25-26).

37. Against the thought that persuades me that we will not be harmed by the sight of a harlot:

> Can anyone bind fire in his bosom and not burn his clothes? Or can anyone walk on coals of fire and not burn his feet? So too the one who goes into a married woman will not be held guiltless (Prov 6:27-29).

38. Against the soul that does not know the reason for temptations and also does not understand that the demon of fornication, whenever it is conquered and departs from us, leaves within us perfect chastity:

> Just as silver and gold are tested in the furnace, so too elect hearts by God (Prov 17:3).[6]

39. Against the unclean thought that entices us and turns us back to that sin for which we have many times repented before the Lord:

> Just as a dog, when it returns to its own vomit, becomes abominable, so is a fool who returns in his wickedness to his own sin (Prov 26:11).

---

[5] That is, John of Lycopolis.
[6] See *To Monks* 60 for this image of testing by fire.

From Qoheleth

40. Against the thought that reminds us of the house in which we gave many fruits to Satan:

    The heart of the wise is in the house of mourning, but the heart of the fool is in the house of mirth (Qo 7:4).

41. Against the soul that is encountering temptations of filthy thoughts and does not want to drive them away with hunger, thirst, keeping vigil, and prayer:

    If the spirit of the ruler rises up against you, do not leave your place, for soothing will put an end to great sins (Qo 10:4).

From the Song of Songs

42. To the holy angels concerning the unclean thoughts that have persisted in the soul:

    Do not look at me, for I am dark, for the sun has looked unfavorably upon me (Song 1:6).

From Job

43. Against the soul that supposes that it is unnatural for it to keep the intellect keen and not to fornicate in its thinking:

    For Job said, "Lest my sons have ever devised evil things against God in their thinking" (Job 1:5).

44. Against the soul that is tested by the demon of fornication with a great unspeakable temptation and marvels at the stupendous temptation to such an extent that this demon is neither put to shame nor feared:

    Is not the life of a human being upon the earth a state of trial and his existence like that of a hired hand by the day? (Job 7:1).[7]

---

[7] Evagrius applies the metaphor of the laborer who is paid daily from Job 7:1 to the gnostic monk in *Reflections* 32.

45. Against the thought that prophesies to me that demons of fornication are coming and will touch our members and set them on fire:

> In the day darkness will come upon them, and let them grope at noon as if it were night (Job 5:14).[8]

46. Against the demon of fornication that compelled Israel to gather straw and reeds instead of grains of wheat:

> Far be it from me to sin before the Lord and to disturb righteousness before the Almighty. Rather, he pays back the human being according to what each of them does (Job 34:10–11).

47. For the soul that does not know from where these burning thoughts are sent against us:

> Out of his [Leviathan's] mouth proceed, as it were, burning lamps (Job 41:11).

From Isaiah[9]

48. Against the thought of fornication that says to me, "I am neither diminished nor destroyed by hunger, thirst, or strenuous fasting":

> But he will destroy your seed with hunger, and he will destroy your remnant (Isa 14:30).

49. Against the demon that advised me in my intellect that I should marry a woman and become the father of sons and so not resist fornicating thoughts with hunger and thirst:[10]

> For the fool will say foolish things, and his heart will think up vain things, in order to perform lawless acts and to speak

---

[8] This is the order in the MS.

[9] This heading is missing in the MS, but appears in 12,175.

[10] The original reading of the MS is "thoughts of fornication," but "fornicating thoughts" is written in the margin of the MS and appears in 12,175 and other Syriac manuscripts (Sims-Williams, *Christian Sogdian Manuscript C2*, 180). The MS reads only "with hunger," but 12,175 reads "with hunger and thirst."

error against the Lord, in order to scatter hungry souls and to make thirsty souls empty (Isa 32:6).

From Jeremiah

50. To the Lord concerning the demons of fornication that take for themselves pretexts from the Scriptures and from the topics that are written in them:

> Lord, who proves righteous deeds and understands guts and hearts, let me see your vengeance upon them, for to you I have revealed my defenses (Jer 20:12).

From the Lamentations of Jeremiah

51. To the Lord concerning the thoughts of fornication that have persisted in me:

> See, Lord, my humiliation, for the enemy has become magnified (Lam 1:9).

52. To the Lord concerning the demon that at night stirred up an accursed thought against my soul and distorted all the features of the face:

> Look, Lord, and see that she has become dishonored (Lam 1:11).

53. Against the soul that has fallen into obscene visions of the night:

> Arise, rejoice in the night at the beginning of your watch; pour out your heart like water before the face of the Lord (Lam 2:19).

54. To the Lord concerning the demon of fornication that, through the passion of desire, imprints in my intellect the vision of an obscene form:

> I called upon your name, Lord, from the lowest dungeon. You heard my voice: do not close your ears to my supplication. You drew near to help me; on the day when I called upon you, you said, "Do not be afraid" (Lam 3:55–57).

From Daniel

55. Against the demon of fornication that, whenever its thoughts ceased, began to explore and touch the body's members—those who have been tempted by this demon will understand what I am saying—those who contend with it should at the time of the attack spend most of the night and day walking in the cell and praying and should catch [only] a little sleep while sitting, and they should wear rough sackcloth and avoid being filled with bread and water; let those who struggle in this contest understand that when by God's power they defeat this demon, they will acquire chastity and not be corrupted:

> And they will drive you forth from human beings, and your dwelling will be with wild beasts, and they will feed you with grass like an ox, and you will lodge under the dew of heaven, and seven times will pass over you, until you know that the Most High rules the kingdom of human beings and will give it to whomever he wishes.[11]

From the Gospel of Matthew

56. Against the intellect that, because of images of men and women[12] that are established in its thinking, is eager to commit a sin:

> Everyone who looks at a woman with lust has already committed adultery with her in his heart (Matt 5:28).[13]

57. Against the soul that is tempted by foul thoughts of fornication and does not want to keep vigil and pray:

> Stay awake and pray that you may not come into temptation (Matt 26:41).

---

[11] Dan 4:25 Theod.

[12] Possibly "images of male and female genitalia."

[13] On the monk using mental images to fantasize about sexual acts, see *Thoughts* 25, also citing Matt 5:28.

The Apostle: From the Letter to the Corinthians

58. Against the thoughts that sometimes lead us to the markets
    and at other times compel us to hang around outside the
    markets:

    > Do not be deceived! Fornicators, idolaters, adulterers, effemi-
    > nate ones, those who lie with men, thieves, the greedy, drunk-
    > ards, revilers, robbers—none of these will inherit the kingdom
    > of God (1 Cor 6:9-10).

59. Against the thoughts that establish in our heart fornication,
    which the Lord sees as having been committed:[14]

    > We must not indulge in fornication as some of them did, and
    > twenty-three thousand fell in a single day (1 Cor 10:8).

From the Letter to the Ephesians

60. Against the unclean thoughts that sometimes hand us over
    to visions of the night and at other times during the day begin
    to depict a vision of images in our intellect:

    > Be sure of this, that no fornicator or impure person, or one
    > who is greedy (that is, an idolater), has any inheritance in the
    > kingdom of Christ and of God (Eph 5:5).

From the Letter of James

61. Against the thought that supposes that temptations come
    upon human beings from God:

    > No one, when tempted, should say, "I am being tempted by
    > God"; for God cannot be tempted by evil and he himself
    > tempts no one. But one is tempted by one's own desire (Jas
    > 1:13-14).

---

[14] See Matt 5:28. The translation accepts the emendation proposed by Frankenberg.

62. Against the soul that does not know that it is due to the desires that every kind of temptation from the demons comes upon it:

> Those conflicts and disputes among you, where do they come from? Do they not come from your desires that are at war within you? (Jas 4:1).

From the Letter of Peter

<63.> Against the soul's thought that does not endure the touch of the demon that suddenly fell between the thighs, moved in them from below, and set [them] on fire:

> Beloved, do not be surprised at the fiery ordeal that is taking place among you to test you, as though something strange were happening to you. But rejoice insofar as you are sharing Christ's sufferings, so that you may also be glad and shout for joy when his glory is revealed (1 Pet 4:12-13).

64. Against the soul's thought that succumbs to distress and sadness and supposes that it is the only one that is tempted so severely:

> Discipline yourselves, keep watch. Like a roaring lion your adversary the devil prowls around, looking for someone to devour. Resist him, steadfast in your faith, for you know that your brothers in all the world are undergoing the same kinds of suffering (1 Pet 5:8-9).

65. Against the thought that threatened me and said, "You are going to suffer from the demons unspeakable evils," which I do not want to set down in writing, lest I hinder the zeal of those who are contending, cast terror into those who have just now withdrawn from the world, and scandalize the inexperienced persons who are in the world; for truly I have

seen the demons[15] perform many unspeakable acts, things
that perhaps it is not lawful to say to most people; for I have
been seized by great astonishment over the patience of the
holy angels, how they have not burned or consumed them
with the flame of the unquenchable fire:

> **The Lord knows how to rescue the godly from trial, and to
> keep the unrighteous under punishment until the day of judg-
> ment** (2 Pet 2:9).

Blessed is our Lord Jesus Christ, our God, who has given us the
victory over the thoughts of the demon of fornication![16]

---

[15] Frankenberg's text mistakenly lacks the plural points, which are present in
the MS.

[16] Frankenberg's text mistakenly lacks "the thoughts of" (*ḥwšbʾ d-*), which
does appear in the MS.

THIRD BOOK

Concerning Love of Money

From Genesis

1. Against the demon that advised me in my thinking, "In a dream I will entice one of your relatives or one of the rich people to send you gold":

   > I stretch out my hand to the most high God, who made heaven and earth, if from a string to a shoe-latchet I take from all that is yours (Gen 14:22-23).[1]

2. Against the thought that shows me bitter poverty and the evils that arise from it and suggests to me that on the day of need I will not find a helper:

   > If the Lord God will be with me, and guard me on this way on which I am going, and give me bread to eat and clothes to wear, and return me safely to the house of my father, then shall the Lord be for me as God, and this stone, which I have set up as a pillar, shall be for me God's house (Gen 28:20-22).

---

[1] The entries in this book are numbered 135 through 191 in 12,175, which lacks 3.8 and 3.10.

From Exodus

3. Against the thought of love of money that made us revile our parents because they did not give us[2] any of their property:

> The one who reviles his father or his mother shall surely die (Exod 21:16).

<4.> Against the thought that, on account of love of money, leads us to afflict with the burden of many labors a brother[3] who has recently become a disciple:

> You shall not afflict the proselyte, for you know the soul of the proselyte. For you yourselves were proselytes in the land of Egypt (Exod 23:9).

From the Book of Leviticus

5. Against the thought of love of money that withheld compassion from a brother who asked out of his need[4] and that advised us to store up for ourselves alone:

> You shall love your neighbor as yourself. I am the Lord (Lev 19:18).

6. Against the thought of love of money that makes us hinder a brother from reading the Scriptures or learning a teaching and that incites us, for the sake of temporary gain, to push him into toil and labor:

> Let no person afflict his neighbor, and you shall fear the Lord your God. For it is I who am the Lord your God (Lev 25:17).

---

[2] MS has "me", but B.L. Add. 12,175 and other Syriac manuscripts have "us" (Sims-Williams, *Christian Sogdian Manuscript C2*, 180).

[3] MS has "the one", but 12,175, other Syriac manuscripts, and the Sogdian have "a brother" (Sims-Williams, *Christian Sogdian Manuscript C2*, 180).

[4] MS has "the one who asked out of need," but 12,175, other Syriac manuscripts, and the Sogdian have "a brother who asked out of his need" (Sims-Williams, *Christian Sogdian Manuscript C2*, 180).

7. Against the thought of love of money that neglects someone who has been sick with a long illness and is greatly afflicted by poverty:[5]

> If your brother who is with you becomes poor and cannot support himself, you shall help him as a stranger and sojourner, and your brother shall live with you (Lev 25:35).

8. Against the thought that demanded more manual labor from a brother than he is capable of:

> Each shall not oppress his brother in labors (Lev 25:46).[6]

From Deuteronomy

9. Against the thought that did not permit us to give to a needy brother who asked to borrow something from us:

> You shall not close your hand to your brother who is in need. You shall open your hands to him and lend him as much as he needs (Deut 15:7-8).

10. Against the thought that seeks to keep resources for itself and does not want to give relief to one of the brothers from them:

> Cursed shall be your barns and your reserves. Cursed shall be the offspring of your belly and the fruits of your land (Deut 28:17-18).[7]

From Judges

11. Against the thought that would increase wealth rather than poverty:

> Is not the gleaning of Ephraim better than the vintage of Abiezer? (Judg 8:2).

---

[5] Frankenberg's text mistakenly lacks the entry number "7" (*z*), which does appear in the MS.

[6] 12,175 lacks this entry.

[7] 12,175 lacks this entry.

From the Book of Kings

12. Against the soul's thought that shows mercy to the poor, but immediately changes its mind and regrets the money that it spent on them:

> Let our hearts be perfect toward the Lord our God, to walk also reverently in his ordinances, and to keep his commandments as this very day (3 Kgdms 8:61).

13. Against the soul that wants to attain the death of Jesus while retaining some wealth and forgets how Elisha the prophet, when he renounced the world, divested himself of all that he had:

> And he departed from there and found Elisha the son of Shaphat, and he was plowing with oxen; there were twelve yoke of oxen before him, and he was with the twelfth. And he passed by him and cast his mantle upon him. And Elisha left the cattle and ran after Elijah and said, "I will kiss my father, and then I will follow you." And Elijah said, "Go back, for I have done [something] for you." And he returned from following him, and took the yoke of oxen, and slew them and boiled them with the instruments of the oxen, and gave them to the people, and they ate. And he arose and went after Elijah and ministered to him (3 Kgdms 19:19-21).

14. Against the soul that is stingy with money and with everything else stored up for it and is unwilling to spend from it on brothers who come:

> And Elisha said to his slave, "Set on the great pot, and boil soup for the sons of the prophets" (4 Kgdms 4:38).

15. Against the soul that has accepted gold that was sent for the business of the brothers and yearns to spend it according to the choice of its own desires, forgetting Gehazi's leprosy—let those reading consider how Elisha the prophet revealed that the thought of love of money is the first of the evil passions, after which follow the rest of the accompanying concepts, from which is generated an extended period of thoughts that hinder the intellect with evil matters and make it leprous:

And Elisha said to him, "Where are you coming from, Gehazi?" And Gehazi said, "Your servant did not go here or there." But Elisha said to him, "Did not my heart go with you when the man came back from his chariot to meet you? And now you accepted silver, and now you have accepted clothing, olive orchards, vineyards, sheep, oxen, and male and female slaves. And Naaman's leprosy shall cleave also to you and to your offspring forever." And he went out from his presence leprous, like snow (4 Kgdms 5:25–27).

From David the Prophet

16. To the Lord concerning the thought of love of money that reminded me by suggesting, "Look, you have given up your parents' inheritance":

> The Lord is the share of my inheritance and of my cup (Ps 15:5).

17. Against the thoughts that taunt us because our parents have forsaken us and will not send us gold to meet our need:

> For my father and my mother have forsaken me, but the Lord has received me (Ps 26:10).

18. Against the thoughts that suggest to us, "Look, your brothers in the world are rich and honored by everyone because of their wealth":

> My soul shall be honored in the Lord; let the meek hear and rejoice (Ps 33:3).

<19>. Against the soul that does not understand that we will be condemned along with Satan unless we rightly administer the possessions that we have been given by God:[8]

---

[8] This entry is not numbered in the manuscript, and it is the only entry between those numbered 18 and 21 in the MS. However, there are two entries numbered 27. Thus, the entries numbered 21–26 and the first "27" must be incorrectly numbered one too high.

> The sinner watches the righteous person and seeks to kill him. But the Lord will not leave him in his hands, nor will he condemn him when he is judged (Ps 36:32–33).

20. Against the soul that clings to the world, loves temporal things, and wants the house and property of its parents:

> Listen, daughter, and see, and incline your ear: forget your people and your father's house. For the King has desired your beauty (Ps 44:11–12).[9]

21. Against the thoughts that meditate upon riches and give no heed to the consuming pain of wealth:

> If wealth should increase, do not set your heart upon it (Ps 61:11).[10]

22. Against the thought that shows us our parents' splendid house and renders our little cell odious in our eyes:

> I would rather be a castoff in the house of God than dwell in the tents of sinners (Ps 83:11).[11]

23. Against the thought that needs money on the pretext of required possessions and has severed its hope from God's grace:

> The Lord will not withhold good things from those who walk in innocence (Ps 83:12).[12]

24. To the Lord concerning the thought of love of money that persists in us and suggests to our intellect either the remembrance of money that we have renounced, or the effort that we are making to acquire things that at present cannot be seen, or the preservation and safekeeping of the things we have now:

---

[9] In the MS this entry is numbered 21.
[10] In the MS this entry is numbered 22.
[11] In the MS this entry is numbered 23.
[12] In the MS this entry is numbered 24.

> Incline my heart to your testimonies and not to covetousness
> (Ps 118:36).[13]

25. Against the thoughts of love of money that depict in me hospitality, compel my soul to take advantage of other people, and incite it to render judgment for the sake of temporal goods:

> The proud have hidden a snare for me, and they have stretched out ropes as snares for my feet; they set a stumbling block for me near the path (Ps 139:6).[14]

26. Against the thought of love of money that prophesies to us that we are going to live in bitter poverty for a long time:

> A human being is like vanity; his days pass by as a shadow (Ps 143:4).[15]

From the Proverbs of Solomon

27. Against the soul that because of the passion of love of money offers scarcely anything for mercy:

> Let not mercy and faith forsake you, but bind them about your neck, and you will find favor. Provide good things before the Lord and human beings (Prov 3:3-4).

28. Against the thought of love of money that prevents us from performing acts of beneficence and suggests to us poverty and bodily infirmity [as excuses]:

> Do not refrain from doing good to the poor whenever it is in your power to help. Do not say, "Come back another time, and tomorrow I will give" (Prov 3:27-28).

29. Against the thought of love of money that, on account of the desire for wealth, drove us to perform manual labor night and

---

[13] In the MS this entry is numbered 25.

[14] Evagrius cites Ps 139:6 also in *Thoughts* 30. In the MS this entry is numbered 26.

[15] In the MS this entry is numbered 27.

day, and so deprived us of reading the Holy Scriptures and
prevented us from visiting and ministering to the sick:

> **Wealth does not profit on the day of wrath, but righteousness
> delivers from death** (Prov 11:4).

30. Against the thought that oppresses us because we are spending
    our money too freely:

> **A man's own wealth is his life's ransom, but a poor person is
> not threatened** (Prov 13:8).

31. Against the thought that, by means of restraint of compassion,
    prefers money to God's wisdom:

> **Wisdom's brood is choicer than gold, prudence's brood choicer
> than silver** (Prov 16:16).

32. Against the thought of love of money that seeks relaxation
    and glory from riches:

> **A good name is better than a lot of wealth, and good favor
> surpasses silver and gold** (Prov 22:1).

33. Against the intellect that is set free from the thoughts of love
    of money through almsgiving, but through sorrow and mur-
    muring is once again ensnared in them—these circumstances
    show that the soul does not discern the passions caused by
    the thoughts nor does it recognize [that they are] fetters for
    the rational nature that strives for knowledge of God:

> **God loves a cheerful and generous man, but he shall complete
> what is lacking of his works** (Prov 22:8a).

From Qoheleth

34. Against the thoughts that remind us of home and property
    and of the way of life associated with them:

> **"Vanity of vanities," said the Preacher, "vanity of vanities: all is
> vanity!"** (Qo 1:2).

35. Against the thought of love of money that both wants to preserve those things that are stored within and wants to collect additional things from without, on the pretexts of refreshment of the brothers and acquisitions of the Holy Scriptures:

> The one who loves silver will not be satisfied with silver, and who has been content with gain in its abundance? This is also vanity (Qo 5:9).

From Job

36. Against the thought that depicted before our eyes the loss of the wealth or property that was of great bodily refreshment to Job:

> The Lord gave, and the Lord took away, as it seemed good to the Lord (Job 1:21).

From Isaiah

37. Against the thought of love of money that advised us to stockpile food and clothing and not to give them to the brothers who need them:

> Break your bread for the hungry person, and bring the poor without shelter into your house. If you see a naked person, clothe him, and do not overlook relatives of your own seed (Isa 58:7).

From the Gospel of Matthew

38. Against the soul that does not yield to mercy when it sees the brothers' poverty:

> Blessed are the merciful, for they will receive mercy (Matt 5:7).

39. Against the soul that wants, because of money or property that has been taken from it, to file a lawsuit, and does not recognize that it will not be set free from the fetters of the

thoughts caused by what has been taken from it unless in love it offers its cloak as well:

> And if anyone wants to sue you and take your coat, give your cloak as well (Matt 5:40).[16]

40. Against the thought that prevented us from lending to a brother on the pretext that he cannot repay:

> Give to everyone who begs from you, and do not refuse anyone who wants to borrow from you (Matt 5:42).

41. Against the inner thoughts that want to acquire riches and to consume the intellect with anxiety about them:

> Do not store up for yourselves treasures on earth, where moth and rust consume and where thieves break in and steal (Matt 6:19).

42. Against the demon that said to us, "Property can, when a person acquires riches, serve the Lord":

> No one can serve two masters; for a slave will either hate the one and love the other, or be devoted to the one and despise the other. You cannot serve God and wealth (Matt 6:24).

43. Against the soul that in a time of distress wants its need to be filled by others, but does not want to refresh others who are afflicted and in want:

> In everything do to others as you would have them do to you; for this is the law and the prophets (Matt 7:12).

From the Gospel of Mark

44. Against the thought that did not permit us to share our wealth when a noble occasion was depicted before our eyes:

> How hard it will be for those who have wealth to enter the kingdom of God! (Mark 10:23).

---

[16] Evagrius explains more fully the dangers of lawsuits, also citing Matt 5:40, in *Thoughts* 32.

The Apostle: From the Letter to the Romans[17]

45. Against the intellect that performed acts of righteousness but
before which was depicted an image of fraud, murmuring,
and sullen faces, things alien to love of practicing the commandments; and that does not want to be troubled by such
passions on account of the holy knowledge that comes to the
intellect when it has been stripped of the foul passions:

> **The compassionate, in cheerfulness. Let love be genuine** (Rom
> 12:8-9).

<From> the Second Letter to the Corinthians

46. Against the thought of love of money that called blessed our
corporeal brothers and our kinfolk who are in the world
because they possess visible wealth:

> **For what can be seen is temporary, but what cannot be seen
> is eternal** (2 Cor 4:18).

47. Against the thought that is sparing in what it gives to the
poor—for giving alms sets the intellect free from thoughts,
while regretting what one has given binds the intellect to the
thoughts that impede it and that damage its ability to receive
the knowledge of God:

> **The point is this: the one who sows sparingly will also reap
> sparingly, and the one who sows bountifully will also reap
> bountifully** (2 Cor 9:6).

From the Letter to the Ephesians

48. Against the thoughts of love of money that corrupt kindness
to the brothers:

> **And be kind to one another, tenderhearted, forgiving one
> another, as God in Christ has forgiven you** (Eph 4:32).

---

[17] The MS reads: "The Apostle: The Letter to the Romans." 12,175 reads:
"From the Letter to the Romans."

From the Letter to the Philippians

49. Against the thought that seeks to store up possessions for itself
    alone:

    > Let each of you look not to your own interests, but to the
    > interests of others (Phil 2:4).

50. Against the thought that presents to us the advantage of
    possessions and displays to us past wealth that would be able
    to support many brothers:

    > Yet whatever gains I had, these I have come to regard as loss
    > because of Christ. More than that, I regard everything as loss
    > because of the surpassing value of knowing Christ Jesus my
    > Lord. For his sake I have suffered the loss of all things, and
    > I regard them as rubbish, in order that I may gain Christ (Phil
    > 3:7-8).

From the Letter to the Colossians[18]

<51.> Against the thoughts that reconcile us to greed and that do
      not see the idolatry that is born from it:

    > Put to death, therefore, whatever in you is earthly: fornication,
    > impurity, passion, evil desire, and greed, which is idolatry. On
    > account of these the wrath of God is coming on those who
    > are disobedient (Col 3:5-6).[19]

From the Letter to the Hebrews

52. Against the thoughts that seek to collect for our need more
    than what we need and that desire to acquire wealth:

    > Keep your lives free from the love of money, and be content
    > with what you have; for he has said, "I will never leave you or
    > forsake you" (Heb 13:5).

---

[18] "From" is lacking in the MS, but appears in 12,175.
[19] Col 3:5 is a favorite verse of Evagrius: see *To Eulogios* 15.15; *Eight Thoughts*
1.30; *Praktikos* Prol.6.

From the First Letter to Timothy

53. Against the soul that seeks more than food and clothing and does not remember that it entered the world bare and it will leave it naked:[20]

> For we brought nothing into the world, so that we can take nothing out of it; but if we have food and clothing, we will be content with these (1 Tim 6:7-8).[21]

54. Against the thought of love of money that said that nothing evil attaches to love of money, but rather great refreshment for the brothers and for strangers [attaches to it]:

> For the love of money is a root of all kinds of evil, and in their eagerness to be rich some have wandered away from the faith and pierced themselves with many pains (1 Tim 6:10).

From the Second Letter to Timothy

55. Against the thought that seeks, on the pretext that profit will fill its need, to be entangled in the affairs of the world:

> No one serving in the army gets entangled in everyday affairs; the soldier's aim is to please the enlisting officer. And in the case of an athlete, no one is crowned without competing according to the rules (2 Tim 2:4-5).

From the Letter of Peter

56. Against the thought that anxiously serves in business affairs on the pretext that the money has run out, and now there is nothing left of it, and it cannot be regained:

---

[20] The MS has "leave it again naked," while 12,175, other Syriac manuscripts, and the Sogdian lack "again" (Sims-Williams, *Christian Sogdian Manuscript C2*, 181).

[21] Evagrius also cites 1 Tim 6:7-8 and 6:10 sequentially at the end of *Thoughts* 21.

Whoever serves must do so with the strength that God sup-
plies, so that God may be glorified in all things through Jesus
Christ (1 Pet 4:11).

From the Letter of John

57. Against the thought of love of money that did not want to
    give alms to the brothers on the pretext that "they are not in
    need" and so in action renounced God's love:

    How does God's love abide in anyone who has the world's
    goods and sees a brother in need and yet refuses help? (1 John
    3:17).

58. Against the thoughts that make us confess in word that we
    love the brothers, while in action we will renounce them
    because of love of money:

    Little children, let us love, not in word or speech, but in truth
    and action (1 John 3:18).

Blessed is our Lord, God, and Savior, Jesus Christ, who has
given us the victory over the demon of love of money, so that we
might defeat it! Amen.

FOURTH BOOK

Concerning the Thoughts of the Demon of Sadness

From Exodus

1. Against the soul that, due to the sadness that comes upon it, thinks that the Lord has not heard its groaning:

   > The children of Israel groaned because of their tasks, and cried, and their cry because of their tasks went up to God. And God heard their groanings (Exod 2:23-24).[1]

2. Against the thoughts that suppose that the Lord does not see our affliction that comes from the demons:

   > And the Lord said to Moses, "I have surely seen the affliction of my people that is in Egypt, and I have heard their cry caused by their taskmasters, for I know their hardship, and I have come down to deliver them out of the hand of the Egyptians" (Exod 3:7-8).

3. Against the soul that does not realize that temptations quickly multiply when it has started to investigate spiritually the living words of God and it has become diligent about God's commandments:

---

[1] The entries in this book are numbered 191 through 267 in 12,175.

Moses turned to the Lord and said, "I pray, Lord, why have you afflicted this people? And why did you send me? For from the time when I went to Pharaoh to speak in your name, he has afflicted this people, and you have not delivered your people" (Exod 5:22-23).

4. Against the thoughts that do not expect to receive help from God and which cast down the soul through sadness:

Speak to the children of Israel, saying, "I am the Lord, and I will lead you out from the tyranny of the Egyptians, and I will deliver you from slavery, and I will ransom you with a raised arm and a great judgment. I will take you to myself as my people, and I will be your God" (Exod 6:6-7).

5. Against the soul that is not convinced that those who have renounced the world only recently will not fall into the hands of the wretched demons and do not fight open attacks through visions or sensation, lest they be alarmed by their [the demons'] terrors and return to the world:[2]

When Pharaoh sent the people out, God did not lead them by the way of the Philistines, although it was near, for God said, "lest at any time the people repent when they see war and return to Egypt" (Exod 13:17).

6. Against the thoughts that say to us, "The demons do not know that the Lord makes war on our behalf":

The Egyptians said, "Let us flee from before Israel, for the Lord makes war on their behalf against the Egyptians" (Exod 14:25).

---

[2] In the *Life of Antony* the devil first attacks Antony with thoughts and only attacks him physically when Antony successfully resists thoughts (*Life of Antony* 5). Later Antony enunciates the general principle that the devil first attacks with thoughts and only later attacks with visions and physical assaults (*Life of Antony* 23).

7. Against the soul that does not know why the demons plot against us:

   > The enemy said, "I will pursue, I will overtake, I will divide the spoils. I will satisfy my soul, I will destroy with my sword, my hand shall rule" (Exod 15:9).

8. To the Lord concerning the thoughts that frighten us by saying, "At night demons will come and fall upon you":

   > Let fear and trembling fall upon them. By the greatness of your arm let them become as stone, until your people pass over, Lord, until your people pass over, which you purchased (Exod 15:16).

9. Against the thoughts of terror that come upon us because the angel who assists us is not visible:

   > With a secret hand the Lord wages war against Amalek from generations to generations (Exod 17:16).

10. Against the soul that is afraid, as if God's angels do not watch over it:

    > And look, I am sending my angel before you, so that it might keep watch over you along the way, so that it might lead you into the land that I have prepared for you (Exod 23:20).

<From Leviticus>

11. Against the soul that is saddened by the tumult of the night and, because of terror, supposes that it will remain in its commotion forever:

    > I will give peace in your land, . . . and you will pursue your enemies, and they will fall before you in slaughter (Lev 26:6-7).[3]

---

[3] Frankenberg's text mistakenly reads the entry number as "10" (γ), but the MS does have "11" (γʹ).

From Deuteronomy[4]

12. Against the human thoughts that consider us and say, "It is of no use for you to fight against the demons":

> And I said to you, "Do not fear, and do not be afraid of them. The Lord your God who goes before you will himself fight alongside you against them" (Deut 1:29-30).

13. Against the soul that has been frightened by the voice of a demon that hissed at it suddenly in the air:

> Begin to inherit it; engage in war with him. In this day I will begin to put the terror and fear of you upon all the nations that are under heaven, who will be troubled when they have heard your name and will be in anguish before you (Deut 2:24-25).

14. Against the human thoughts that are terrified by the vision of a demon whose eyes flash like fire:

> Do not be afraid of them. The Lord your God who goes before you will himself fight alongside you against them (Deut 1:29-30).

15. To the Lord concerning the soul that remained undisturbed when suddenly demons fell upon the body with noise and tumult:[5]

> Lord, Lord, you have begun to show to your servant your strength, your power, your mighty hand, and your high arm, for what god is there in heaven or on earth who will do as you have done and according to your might? (Deut 3:24).

16. Against the soul that is frightened and scared by the demons that appear to it and supposes that the Lord has abandoned it:

---

[4] "From" is missing in the MS, but appears in 12,175.

[5] The several references to bodily attacks by the demons in this book are distinctive within the Evagrian corpus, but Evagrius does mention such attacks elsewhere, e.g., in *Chapters on Prayer* 91.

> The Lord your God will not abandon you, nor will he destroy you; he will not forget the covenant of your fathers, which the Lord swore to them (Deut 4:31).

17. Against the soul that wants to know the reason for these trials:

> . . . so that he might afflict you and test you and treat you well at the end of your days (Deut 8:16).

18. Against the human thoughts that are frightened by the vision of demons that come to us at night twisted like snakes on one's back and side:

> Do not let your heart become faint; do not be afraid; do not tremble, and do not turn away from them, for it is the Lord your God who advances with you, to wage war with you against your enemies so as to rescue you (Deut 20:3-4).

19[a]. Against the soul that is saddened and frightened by the demons that come upon it suddenly at night:

> Be courageous and strong; do not fear or be cowardly; do not be afraid before them. For it is the Lord your God who advances with you and among you, who will not forsake you or abandon you (Deut 31:6).[6]

From Joshua, Son of Nun

[19b.] Against the soul that wants, through its withdrawal from the world, to grow strong in the fear of God, but is hindered by the fear that comes from the demons:

> Be strong and courageous; do not be cowardly or afraid. For the Lord your God is with you wherever you may go (Josh 1:9).[7]

---

[6] In the MS this entry is numbered simply "19."

[7] This entry is not numbered in the MS.

20. Against the thoughts that hesitate to undertake the life of fear of God out of fear of the frightening visions and lamps of fire that fly through the air:

> Do not be afraid of them, and do not be cowardly . . . for thus the Lord will do to all your enemies against whom you wage war (Josh 10:25).

From Judges[8]

21. Against the soul that succumbs to sadness and therefore is frightened by visions of the night:

> Wake up, wake up, Deborah! Wake up, wake up, and sing a song! Get up, Barak, and lead your captivity captive, son of Abinoam! (Judg 5:12).

From Samuel

22. Against the soul[9] that does not know that the melody that accompanies the Psalms alters the condition of the body and drives away the demon that touches it on the back, chills its sinews, and troubles all its members:[10]

> And it happened that when the evil spirit was upon Saul, David took his harp and played with his hand, and Saul was refreshed, and it was good with him, and the evil spirit departed from him (1 Kgdms 16:23).

23. Against the demon that appears carrying a sword—we should, as in a hostile manner, answer back with a phrase, just as our blessed father Abba Macarius answered it when he saw it

---

[8] "From" is missing in the MS, but appears in 12,175.

[9] Frankenberg"s text reads "thought" (*mḥšbtʾ*), which is the original reading of the MS, but an ancient corrector marked the word and wrote in the margin "soul" (*npšʾ*), which is also the reading of 12,175.

[10] Compare Athanasius, *Epistle to Marcellinus* 28, discussed briefly in the Introduction.

carrying a sword and coming to attack him when he had traveled to see the paradise that Jannes and Jambres made:[11]

> You come to me with a sword and a spear and a shield, but I come to you in the name of the Lord God of hosts (1 Kgdms 17:45).

24. Against the demons that make a commotion in the air and then make us listen to their voices:

> Not with a sword or spear does the Lord deliver, for the battle belongs to the Lord, and the Lord will deliver you into our hands (1 Kgdms 17:47).

25. Against the demon that threatens me with curses and said, "I will make you an object of laughter and reproach among all the monks because you have investigated and made known all the kinds of all the unclean thoughts":

> That's enough! Let not the humpbacked one boast like the one that is upright! (3 Kgdms 21:11).

From the Book of Kings

26. Against the soul that is frightened by the demons that appear suddenly in the air:

> Do not be afraid, for those that are with us outnumber those that are with them (4 Kgdms 6:16).

---

[11] On Jannes and Jambres see 2 Tim 3:8. The phrase "blessed father Macarius" in the MS and 12,175 is most likely a mistake for "holy father Macarius," which is how Evagrius normally names Macarius the Alexandrian, who is the Macarius to whom he refers here: see Antoine Guillaumont, "Le problème des deux Macaire dans les *Apophthegmata Patrum*," *Irénikon* 47 (1974): 41–59, at 52. For other accounts of this incident or a similar one, sometimes involving Macarius the Great (or the Egyptian), see *History of the Monks of Egypt (Historia monachorum in Aegypto)* 21.5–12; Palladius, *Lausiac History* 18.5–9; *Sayings of the Desert Fathers* Macarius the Great 2. Evagrius mentions the appearance of a sword-bearing demon also in *Chapters on Prayer* 92.

27. Against the soul that does not believe that the air is filled with holy angels that help us and are not visible to the demons:

> Elisha prayed and said, "Lord, open the eyes of the servant, and let him see." And the Lord opened his eyes, and he saw. And look, the mountain was filled with horses, and there were chariots of fire encircling Elisha (4 Kgdms 6:17).

From David[12]

28. Against the thought that cast me into fear and trembling on the pretext that demons are coming and fighting with me:

> The one who dwells in the heavens will laugh them to scorn, and the Lord will mock them. Then he will speak to them in his anger, and in his fury he will trouble them (Ps 2:4-5).

29. To the Lord concerning the disordered and foul visions that appear to us at night:

> Have mercy upon me, Lord, for I am weak; heal me, Lord, for my bones are troubled. My soul is greatly troubled, and as for you, Lord, how long? Return, Lord, and deliver my soul; save me for your mercy's sake (Ps 6:3-5).

30. Against the thoughts that advise us to flee from before the demons' evil and not to oppose them valiantly in the contest:

> In the Lord I have placed my trust. How will you say to my soul, "Flee to the mountains as a sparrow"? (Ps 10:1).

31. To the Lord concerning the expectation that demons are about to come upon us at night:

> Rise up, Lord, and prevent them, and cast them down. Deliver my soul from the ungodly, your sword from the enemies of your hand (Ps 16:13).

32. Against the soul that is disturbed by the tumultuous sounds and commotion of the demons:

---

[12] Frankenberg's text mistakenly reads "from the same" (*mn hw*) while the MS has "from David" (*mn dwyd*). 12,175 reads: "From the Psalms of David."

> Some glory in chariots and some in horses, but we will glory
> in the name of the Lord our God. They are overthrown and
> fallen, but we have arisen and have been set upright (Ps
> 19:8-9).

33. Against the demons that touch our bodies at night and like
    scorpions strike our limbs:

> The Lord is my light and my savior; whom shall I fear? The
> Lord is the defender of my life; of whom shall I be afraid?
> (Ps 26:1).

34. Against the demons that suddenly appear to us out of the air
    like Ethiopians:[13]

> If an army arrays itself against me, my heart shall not fear;
> if war arises against me, in this I have hope (Ps 26:3).

35. To the Lord concerning the demon of sadness that approached
    me and that alone [among the demons] did not create a desire,
    but whose entire work was in the head and in the back;
    having introduced sadness with thoughts, it then no longer
    required thoughts, but cast the soul into great and unneces-
    sary distress:

> You are my refuge from the affliction that surrounds me, my
> joy, to deliver me from those that encircle me (Ps 31:7).

---

[13] The Syriac word here (*hndwy*) normally refers to "Indians," but the important concept here is the black skin in which the demons appear, and thus it
is virtually certain that Evagrius wrote "Ethiopians," the archetypal black-skinned
persons in his Egyptian context (rather than in the Syrian context of the translator). A similar change appears in the Syriac version of the *Life of Antony*, which
calls the black demon that appears to Antony in chapter 6 an "Indian" (*hndwy*)
(R. Draguet, *La vie primitive de S. Antoine conservée en syriaque*, Corpus Scriptorum
Christianorum Orientalium 417–18 [Leuven: Peeters, 1980] 1:16–17). The
warlike nature of Ethiopians, suggested here by the citation of Ps 26:3, appears
in other early monastic works. On black or Ethiopian demons, see David Brakke,
"Ethiopian Demons: Male Sexuality, the Black-Skinned Other, and the Monastic
Self," *Journal of the History of Sexuality* 10 (2001): 501–35, and *Demons and the
Making of the Monk: Spiritual Combat in Early Christianity* (Cambridge, MA:
Harvard University Press, 2006), 157–81.

36. To the Lord concerning the demons that fall upon the skin of the body, put branding marks in it as if made by fire, and make visible marks in it as if made by a cupping-glass—things that I have seen many times with my own eyes and at which I have marveled:

> Judge, Lord, those who do me injustice; make war against those who make war against me. Take hold of a shield and buckler, and rise up for my help. Bring forth a sword, and stop the way against those that persecute me. Say to my soul, "I am your salvation" (Ps 34:1-3).

37. To the Lord concerning the demon of sadness that alters the intellect and impresses it with a single concept that is filled with severe grief—this is an indication of great madness:

> Deliver my soul from their wickedness, my only-begotten one from the lions (Ps 34:17).

38. Against the thought that threatens me and said, "Look, at night demons will come, carrying swords":

> Let their sword enter into their own heart, and let their bows be broken (Ps 36:15).

39. Against the thought that prophesies to me concerning the scourge that comes from demons:

> For I am ready for scourges, and my grief is continually before me (Ps 37:18).

40. Against the soul that, in the time of sadness, wants to find in prayer spiritual words:

> Do not forsake me, Lord; my God, do not depart from me. Come near to help me, Lord of my salvation (Ps 37:22-23).

41. To the Lord concerning the demons that burned the body's sinews:

> Take from me your scourges; from the strength of your hand I have fainted (Ps 38:11).

42. Against the soul concerning the thought of sadness that depicted before our eyes our father's old age, our mother's lack of strength, and the sorrow of our relatives, who are not comforted:

> His words are smoother than oil, but they are darts (Ps 54:22).

43. To the Lord concerning the demon that in my intellect threatens me with madness and mental illness, to the shame of me and of those who seek the Lord through the monastic life:

> Do not let those who wait on you, Lord of hosts, be ashamed on my account. Do not let those who seek you, God of Israel, be embarrassed because of me (Ps 68:7).

44. Against the soul that does not understand what the leaders of the demons say about persons who have been "abandoned by the Lord":

> For my enemies have spoken against me, and those that would possess my soul have taken counsel together, saying, "God has abandoned him. Pursue him and seize him, for he has no deliverer" (Ps 70:10–11).

45. To the Lord concerning the serpents that appear flying in the air and also make themselves come out of the walls—we should say what the ancient Egyptian, the blessed Macarius, opened his mouth and said:

> Do not hand over to the beasts a soul that confesses you (Ps 73:19).

46. Against the soul that is not convinced that the filthy demons talk to one another about us:

> They have said, "Come, and let us destroy them out of the nation, and let the name of Israel no longer be remembered" (Ps 82:5).

47. Against the demons that gradually begin to imitate obscene images and to appear out of the air—we should answer with a phrase, as also the righteous blessed Antony answered and said:

> The Lord is my helper, and I shall look upon my enemies (Ps 117:7).[14]

48. Against the demon that burst into flame like a fire and then dissolved again into smoke:

> The snare has been broken, and we have been delivered. Our help is in the name of the Lord, who made heaven and earth (Ps 123:7-8).

49. To the Lord concerning the demon that threatens to burn me with a flaming fire:

> Coals will fall upon them, and you will cast them down into fire; in hardships they will not bear up (Ps 139:11).[15]

From the Proverbs of Solomon

50. Against the thought that said to me, "The path that leads to knowledge of Jesus Christ is full of great danger and much affliction":

> The timid person makes excuses and says, "There is a lion in the paths and murderers in the streets" (Prov 22:13).

[14] So in the *Life of Antony* Antony responds to the black boy who appears to him as "the spirit of fornication" shortly after the devil has appeared to Antony as a woman (Athanasius, *Life of Antony* 6.4). Evagrius alludes to Ps 117:7 in the context of demonic appearances also in *Chapters on Prayer* 92.

[15] MS: "Coals of fire will fall upon them. They will fall down in fire and not be able to bear up."

From Job

51. Against the soul that does not know that Satan cannot approach even cattle without God's command:

> You have blessed the works of his hand, and you have made his cattle numerous upon the land. But stretch out your hand, and touch all that he has, and [see] whether truly he will bless you to your face (Job 1:10–11).

52. Against the soul that does not understand that, after the trials that it has through thoughts, Satan sets to work and requests of God that he be given authority over the body:[16]

> The devil answered and said to the Lord, "Skin for skin, as much as a person has he will give as a ransom for his soul. No, rather, stretch out your hand, and touch his bones and his flesh, and [see] whether truly he will bless you to your face" (Job 2:4–5).

53. Against the thoughts that frighten us by prophesying to us and saying, "Look, at night demons will come like stars and appear in the cell and burn your eyes and face"—it is expedient for us at that moment of trial to kneel, to persist in prayer, to turn away our face, and not to look when they are trying to disturb us:

> Let the stars of that night be darkened; let [that night] remain dark and not come into light, and let it not see the morning star rise (Job 3:9).

54. Against the thought that prophesies to me and said, "Death will come to you from the demons":

> For if a human being should die, will he live again after having completed the days of his life? (Job 14:14).

---

[16] For the sequence of thoughts followed by bodily attacks, see 4.5 and Athanasius, *Life of Antony* 5, 23. The idea that Satan must ask God's permission to attack the monk's body comes from Job 2:4–6, where God must grant Satan the power to touch Job's body.

From Micah

55. Against the evil spirit that opposes my soul, introduces and displays to me sins of the past, and tries to cast sadness into it [my soul]:

> Do not rejoice over me, my enemy, because I have fallen. I shall rise up, for if I sit in darkness, the Lord serves as a light for me (Mic 7:8).

From Nahum

56. Against the soul that does not valiantly withstand the demon that at the time of prayer suddenly comes, lands on the shoulders[17] and neck, scratches the ears, and punches the nose:

> The Lord is kind to those who wait upon him on the day of affliction, knowing those who show him reverence (Nah 1:7).

<From Zechariah>

57. Against the soul that wants to learn what is to happen to the demons on the day of judgment and what is the generation of torment to which they are to be handed over—concerning this torment the prophet, prophesying mystically, narrated and said:

> And this is the overthrow with which the Lord will strike all the nations that fought against Jerusalem: their flesh will rot away while they are standing on their feet, and their eyes will melt out of their sockets, and their tongue will rot away in their mouth (Zech 14:12).

---

[17] MS: "wings."

From Isaiah

58. Against the demons that suddenly emitted fire and disturbed with alarming sounds—because they cast the soul into a stupor, we should not let it [the soul] fall into their terror, but we should say what our holy father Macarius also answered against them and said:

> Know, you nations, and be conquered; listen, even to the end of the earth. Having become strong, be conquered. For even if you become strong again, you will be conquered again. And whatever counsel you should take, the Lord will bring it to naught; and whatever word you speak, it shall not endure, for God is with us (Isa 8:9–10).

59. Against the thoughts that come to us because of the weakness that the demons create in us:

> I do not disobey, nor do I dispute. I gave my back to scourges and my cheek to blows. I did not turn my face away from the shame of spitting, but the Lord God was my helper (Isa 50:5–7).[18]

60. Against the soul's thought that saddens it because of the contempt that it receives when friends and relatives reproach it for not having distributed to them from its wealth, and in turn it receives no consolation from them:

> Do not fear the reproach of human beings, and do not be overcome by their contempt (Isa 51:7).

61. Against the soul that does not understand that empty thoughts give birth within it to fear and trembling, and they obscure the holy light that confidence gives to the intellect:

> Abstain from injustice, and you will not be afraid, and trembling will not come near to you (Isa 54:14).

---

[18] The heading "From Jeremiah" incorrectly appears before this entry in the MS, but not so in 12,175.

From Jeremiah[19]

62. Against the soul that is frightened by the flashes of lightning that happen on the walls:

> Do not be afraid before them, for I am with you to rescue you, says the Lord (Jer 1:8).

63. To the Lord concerning the thoughts of sadness that lead the intellect to an abyss filled with dead persons and that imprint in the heart obscene visions—this is an indication of a soul that has fallen into danger:

> Why do those who sadden me prevail against me? My wound is severe: from where will I receive healing? It has indeed become for me like deceitful water, which has no trustworthiness (Jer 15:18).

64. To the Lord concerning the demons that say to us in our intellect, "Soon you will be put to shame in your way of life":

> Let those who persecute me be put to shame, but do not let me be put to shame. Let them be alarmed, but do not let me be alarmed. Bring upon them the evil day; crush them with double destruction (Jer 17:18).

From Ezekiel

65. Against the soul that is frightened by the attacks of demons that happen through touching:

> Do not be afraid of them, nor be alarmed before them, because it is a house of provocateurs (Ezek 3:9).

---

[19] This heading actually appears incorrectly before no. 59 in the MS, but it appears correctly here in 12,175.

From the Gospel of Matthew

66. Against the soul that is not convinced that the demons do not have authority even over swine, even though they boast, "We have authority over human beings, and we enslave them according to our will":

> Now a large herd of swine was feeding at some distance from them. The demons begged him, "If you cast us out, send us into the herd of swine." And he said to them, "Go!" (Matt 8:30–32).

From the Gospel of John

67. Against the soul that does not understand that weakness of faith brings trepidation and fear into the heart:

> Do not let your hearts be troubled. Have faith in God, have faith also in me (John 14:1).

From Acts

68. Against the soul that is sad because it has suffered dishonor for the sake of the Lord's name:

> As they left the council, they rejoiced that they were considered worthy to suffer dishonor for the sake of the name (Acts 5:41).

From the Letter to the Romans

69. Concerning the suffering that comes from temptations:

> And not only that, but we also boast in our sufferings, knowing that suffering produces endurance, and endurance produces character, and character produces hope, and hope does not disappoint us, because God's love has been poured into our hearts through the Holy Spirit that has been given to us (Rom 5:3–5).

70. Against the thought that prophesies to me severe sufferings that come from temptations:

> I consider that the sufferings of the present time are not worth comparing with the glory about to be revealed to us (Rom 8:18).

From the First Letter to the Corinthians

71. Against the soul's thought that supposes that it is tested beyond its strength:

> God is faithful, and he will not let you be tested beyond your strength, but with the testing he will also provide the way out so that you may be able to endure it (1 Cor 10:13).

From the Second Letter to the Corinthians

72. Against the soul, concerning a stupefying, indescribable temptation, which I do not want to reveal in words because of those people who, whether out of malice or out of ignorance, ridicule with both careful and careless words and who suppose that demons do not harass monks openly—these are persons who have no experience at all of the warfare of those demons that, through a request made of God, have received the authority to test us:

> Indeed, we felt that we had received the sentence of death so that we would rely not on ourselves but on God who raises the dead. He who rescued us from so deadly a peril will continue to rescue us (2 Cor 1:9-10).

73. Against the demon that brings to me the sins of my youth:

> Everything old has passed away; see, everything has become new (2 Cor 5:17).

74. Against the thoughts of sadness that come to us concerning transitory affairs, sinking the intellect into great affliction and killing it:[20]

> For godly grief produces a repentance that leads to salvation and brings no regret, but worldly grief produces death (2 Cor 7:10).[21]

From the Letter of James

75. Against the thoughts of the soul that is joined in open warfare against the demons:

> Submit yourselves therefore to God. Resist the devil, and he will flee from you (Jas 4:7).

From the Letter of Peter

76. Against the thoughts that expect the soul to be wounded by demons and the body to fall into incurable illness:

> Now who will harm you if you are eager to do what is good? But even if you do suffer for doing what is right, you are blessed. Do not fear what they fear, and do not be intimidated, but in your hearts sanctify Christ as Lord (1 Pet 3:13–15).

Blessed is our Lord God and Savior Jesus Christ, who has given us the victory over the demon of sadness!

---

[20] Here Evagrius alludes to sadness that stems from the frustration of desires: see *Praktikos* 10, 19.

[21] Evagrius discusses these two types of sadness ("godly grief" and "worldly grief") in *To Eulogios* 7; see also *Eight Thoughts* 5.19.

FIFTH BOOK
Against the Demon of Anger

From the Book of Genesis

1. Against the soul that does not know that a gift readily extinguishes a brother's long-standing grudge:

   Jacob said, "If I have found favor before you, receive the gifts from my hands. For this reason I have seen your face, as someone might see the face of God, and you will be pleased with me. Receive my blessings that I have brought to you, because God has been merciful to me and is everything to me" (Gen 33:10-11).[1]

2. Against the thoughts of anger that arise along the way of righteous living:

   Do not get angry along the way (Gen 45:24).

From Exodus[2]

3. Against the thought of bearing false witness that is born of anger:

   You shall not bear false witness against your neighbor (Exod 20:16).

---

[1] The entries in this book are numbered 267 through 329 in 12,175, which mistakenly uses the numbers 267 and 269 twice.

[2] This heading is missing in the MS, but appears in 12,175.

119

4. Against the thought that came from a slanderer and that arouses and stirs up rage against the brothers:

   You shall not accept an idle rumor (Exod 23:1).

5. Against the thought that is stirred up by anger and wants to revile the brothers:

   You shall abstain from every unjust word (Exod 23:7).

\<From Leviticus\>

6. Against the thought that depicted in the intellect a brother who in hatred said something wicked or listened to something hateful—this is like what John the prophet, the seer of Thebes, used to report, "It is possible for this hatred not to continue if it has to do with wealth or food, but hatred on account of the glory that comes from human beings is difficult to uproot":

   You shall not hate your brother in your thinking. But with a reproof rebuke your neighbor, and you will not take on sin because of him (Lev 19:17).

From Numbers

7. Against the soul that thinks that perfect humility is beyond [human] nature:

   And the human being Moses was very meek, beyond all the human beings that were upon the earth (Num 12:3).[3]

From Samuel

8. Against the soul that does not understand that revilings from human beings occur when God hands it over to be tested:

   David said to Abishai and to all his slaves, "Look, my son who came forth from my bowels seeks my soul, and also now the

---

[3] For Moses as a model of gentleness, see *Thoughts* 13.

son of Benjamin. Let him revile, because the Lord has spoken
to him. If somehow the Lord looks upon my lowliness, he will
return to me good things instead of his reproaches on the
last day" (2 Kgdms 16:11–12).[4]

From David

9. Against the soul that has neglects humility but longs to learn
the ways of the Lord:

> He will guide the meek in judgment; he will teach the meek
> his ways (Ps 24:9).[5]

10. Against the soul that accepts thoughts of anger and collects
against the brothers wicked pretexts and false suspicions:

> Cease from anger, and forsake wrath; do not be anxious, so
> that you do evil. For the evildoers shall be destroyed, but
> those who wait for the Lord, they shall inherit the earth
> (Ps 36:8–9).[6]

11. Against the thought that is set in motion by slander of the
brothers and that obscures the soul with a cloud of rage:

> Sitting, you slander your brother, and against your mother's
> son you have placed a stumbling block (Ps 49:20).

<12.> To the Lord because the intellect realized that frightening
visions in the night come from the tumult of rage, and it
understood as well that they are extinguished through mercy
and patience:

> You have made me wise in your commandment beyond my
> enemies, for it is mine forever. I have understood more than
> all my teachers, for your testimonies are my meditation (Ps
> 118:98–99).

---

[4] Evagrius cites David's restraint in this episode also in *To Eulogios* 4.4.
[5] See *Thoughts* 13.
[6] See *Thoughts* 5.

13. Against the demon that provokes anger against the brothers
    and also persuades us to chant this psalm, where is written
    the command to be patient, which we do not keep—it [the
    demon] does this in order to mock us as we speak that com-
    mandment which we do not keep in action:

    > How shall we sing the Lord's song in a foreign land? (Ps
    > 136:4).

From the Proverbs of Solomon

14. Against the thought that collects wicked ideas against a
    brother, for example, that he is negligent or he is a reviler or
    he does not do what he ought:

    > Do not devise evil things against your friend, who lives near
    > you and trusts in you (Prov 3:29).

15. Against the thought that came from hatred and wanted to
    quarrel with a brother about transitory affairs:

    > Hatred stirs up strife, but love covers all who do not love
    > strife (Prov 10:12).

16. Against the thought that compelled us to pronounce a curse
    against a brother:

    > Righteous lips cover enmity, but those who pronounce curses
    > are extremely foolish (Prov 10:18).

17. Against the anger that is agitated against a brother and at the
    time of prayer makes the intellect unseemly:

    > Every blessed soul is sincere, but an angry man is unseemly
    > (Prov 11:25).[7]

18. Against the thought that arouses our anger against cattle that
    do not go straight on their path:

    > A righteous person pities the souls of his cattle, but the feel-
    > ings of the ungodly are unmerciful (Prov 12:10).

---

[7] For the entry number Frankenberg's text mistakenly has only *z*, while the
MS does have *yz*.

19. Against the thought that is quickly aroused by anger and, based on a trivial pretext, agitates the intellect:

    A fool immediately announces his anger, but a clever man conceals his disgrace (Prov 12:16).

20. Against the thought that thinks up treachery against a brother:

    A treacherous person will not catch game, but a pure man is a precious possession (Prov 12:27).

21. Against the soul that marches on the way of resentment and, by means of thoughts, drags the intellect along, so that the intellect becomes enflamed with anger, and even after the thought of this passion subsides and some time has passed, there remains a representation of a word or transitory matter that clouds and imprints the intellect:

    In the ways of righteousness is life, but the ways of those who carry resentments lead to death (Prov 12:28).[8]

22. Against the thought of anger that disturbs and uproots patience and makes us consider acts of folly, the power of which comes from the desire for possessions and instead of which humility ought to be aroused:

    The patient man abounds in understanding, but the impatient one is very foolish (Prov 14:29).

23. Against the thought of anger that prevents us from answering with humility those who chastise us rightly:

    Anger destroys even wise persons; a submissive answer turns away anger, but a painful word raises up anger (Prov 15:1).

24. Against the thought that provokes us to strife with the brothers and prevents us from cutting off arguments:

    An irascible man prepares arguments, but a patient one soothes an argument that is just starting (Prov 15:18).

---

[8] For a brief discussion of the process by which representations come to imprint the intellect, see the Introduction. Evagrius cites Prov 12:28 in his discussion of the resentment exacerbated by lawsuits in *Thoughts* 32.

25. Against the soul that supposes that it is not the thought of anger that is an abomination before God, but only the sin that results from it:

> An unrighteous thought is an abomination to the Lord, but words of the pure ones are holy (Prov 15:26).

26. Against the thought that advised us to love angry people and words of wrath:

> Do not be a companion to an irascible man, and do not lodge with an angry friend, lest you learn his ways and receive snares for your soul (Prov 22:24–25).

27. Against the soul that has suffered wrong and wants to do wrong as well—this is an indication of an evil passion belonging to a soul that loves vain things:

> Do not say, "As he has treated me, I will treat him, and I will repay him the wrong he has done me" (Prov 24:29).

28. Against the intellect that is not merciful, does not have pity on its enemy when it sees him in bitter poverty, and does not want to dissolve his enmity with a meal:

> If your enemy is hungry, feed him, and if he is thirsty, give him drink. For by doing this you will heap hot coals upon his head, and the Lord will reward you with good things (Prov 25:21–22).

From Qoheleth

29. Against the soul's thought that is quickly enflamed with anger and is swiftly embittered against the brothers:

> Do not be quick in your spirit to become angry, for anger rests in the breast of the foolish (Qo 7:9).

30. Against the soul that does not want to let go of pretexts for anger, but desires food, clothing, riches, and the glory that passes away; anger that is stirred up on account of these things does not depart from the heart, but rather plunges the intellect into the depths of perdition:

> Remove anger from your heart, and take evil from your flesh, for youth and folly are vanity (Qo 11:10).[9]

From the Song of Songs

31. Against the demon that seeks through many temptations to extinguish our love for the brothers:

> Much water will not be able to extinguish love, and rivers will not drown it (Song 8:7).

From Isaiah

32. Against the thought that provokes me to write to the person who has caused us trouble harmful words that will strike his heart:

> Woe to those who write evil, for it is by writing that they write evil (Isa 10:1).

From the Lamentations of Jeremiah

33. To the Lord concerning thoughts of anger that no longer provoke us:

> You have judged, Lord, the causes of my soul; you have redeemed my life. You saw my troubles; you have judged my case. You have seen all their vindictiveness; [you have seen] into all their thoughts against me (Lam 3:58-60).

[9] See *Thoughts* 5.

From the Gospel of Matthew

34. Against the thoughts of anger that our parents and siblings present to us at the time when they persecute us on account of the Lord's name:

> Blessed are those who are persecuted for righteousness' sake, for theirs is the kingdom of heaven (Matt 5:10).

35. Against the thought that is agitated against a brother due to listlessness:

> If you are angry with a brother, you will be liable to judgment (Matt 5:22).

36. Against the intellect that has become angry with someone who struck it and, because of a second strike, does not want to let go of the thought that came because of the original strike:

> If anyone strikes you on the right cheek, turn the other also (Matt 5:39).

37. Against the thoughts that provoke us to hate and curse our enemies:

> Love your enemies, and pray for those who persecute you, so that you may be children of your Father in heaven (Matt 5:44-45).

From the Gospel of Luke

38. Against the thought of anger that is not satisfied with a brother's repentance but rather becomes newly embittered against him:

> If your brother sins, you must rebuke him, and if he repents, you must forgive him. And if he sins against you seven times a day, and turns back to you seven times and says, "I repent," you must forgive (Luke 17:3-4).

From the Gospel of John

39. Against the intellect that accepts thoughts of anger against the brothers and perverts the commandment of love, which is called "new":

> I give you a new commandment, that you love one another. Just as I have loved you, you also should love one another (John 13:34).

From the Letter to the Romans

40. Against the thoughts of anger that are embittered against love:

> Who will separate us from the love of Christ? Will hardship, or distress, or persecution, or famine, or nakedness, or peril, or sword? (Rom 8:35).

41. Against the thoughts of envy that rejoice in the misfortune of our enemies:

> Rejoice with those who rejoice; weep with those who weep. Live in harmony with one another (Rom 12:15–16).

42. Against the thought that holds a grudge and endeavors to repay evil to the one who grieved it:

> Do not repay anyone evil for evil, but take thought for what is noble in the sight of all (Rom 12:17).

From the First Letter to the Corinthians

43. Against the thoughts of anger that advise us to take advantage and to defraud:

> Why not rather be wronged? Why not rather be defrauded? But you yourselves wrong and defraud—and brothers at that (1 Cor 6:7).

44. Against the thought of anger that becomes enraged against someone who taunted us about [our] slavery:

> Were you a slave when called? Do not be concerned about it. If you can become free, avail yourself of the opportunity. For whoever was called in the Lord as a slave is a freed person belonging to the Lord (1 Cor 7:21-22).

45. Against the soul that is not permitted the frank speech of love but is deprived of it by a thought of anger:

> If I speak in the tongues of mortals and of angels, but do not have love, I am a noisy gong or a clanging cymbal. And if I have prophetic powers, and understand all mysteries, and all knowledge, and if I have all faith, so as to remove mountains, but do not have love, I am nothing. If I give away all my possessions, and if I hand over my body so that I may boast, but do not have love, I gain nothing. Love is patient; love is kind; love is not envious or boastful or arrogant or rude. It does not insist on its own way; it is not irritable or resentful; it does not rejoice in any wrongdoing, but rejoices in the truth. It bears all things, believes all things, hopes all things, endures all things. Love never ends (1 Cor 13:1-8).

From the Letter to the Galatians

46. Against the soul that is swiftly angry but wants to find within itself the frontier of the knowledge of truth:

> The fruit of the Spirit is love, joy, peace, patience, kindness, generosity, faithfulness, gentleness, and self-control (Gal 5:22-23).

47. Against the thoughts that cast us into grief over the brothers' failings:

> Bear one another's burdens, and in this way you fulfill the law of Christ (Gal 6:2).

48. Against the soul's thoughts that feed on anger against someone who received many good things from us and then complained about them:[10]

> So let us not grow weary in doing what is right, for we will reap at harvest time, if we do not give up (Gal 6:9).

From the Letter to the Ephesians

49. Against the thoughts of anger that do not permit us to be reconciled to the brothers because they depict before our eyes pretexts that are "suitable" yet actually are shame, fear, and pride—"Did he not fall into the very same offenses as earlier, he who transgressed in this matter?"—this is an indication of the craftiness of the demon, which does not want to let the intellect become free of resentment:

> Do not let the sun go down on your anger, and do not make room for the devil (Eph 4:26-27).

50. Against the thoughts of any kind that are born of anger about matters of different sorts:

> Put away from you all bitterness and wrath and anger and wrangling and slander, together with all malice (Eph 4:31).

<From> the Letter to the Philippians

51. Against the thoughts of anger that dare to murmur about service to the brothers:

> Do all things without murmuring and arguing, so that you may be blameless and innocent, children of God without blemish, in the midst of a crooked and perverse generation (Phil 2:14-15).

---

[10] The MS and 12,175 read: "many good things from them." 12,175 has the correct masculine singular form of "complained" (*rṭn*) while the MS has the plural (*rṭnw*).

From the Letter to the Colossians

52. Against the thoughts that derive from enflamed anger and that, from their heat, give birth to blasphemy and treachery:

> But now you must get rid of all such things—anger, wrath, malice, slander, and abusive language from your mouth. Do not lie to one another (Col 3:8-9).

From the First Letter to the Thessalonians[11]

53. Against the thoughts that want to repay evil for evil:

> See that none of you repays evil for evil, but always seek to do good to one another and to all (1 Thess 5:15).

From the First Letter to Timothy

54. Against the soul that does not know the aim of God's commandment and, because of thoughts of anger, perverts it:

> The aim of such instruction is love that comes from a pure heart, a good conscience, and sincere faith (1 Tim 1:5).

From the Second Letter to Timothy

55. Against the intellect that by means of thoughts stirs up conflict in its thinking:

> The Lord's slave must not be quarrelsome, but kindly to everyone (2 Tim 2:24).

56. Against the thought of anger that happens to me because of persecution, when I am persecuted by my parents and my relatives because of the Lord's name:

> All who want to live a godly life in Christ Jesus will be persecuted (2 Tim 3:12).

---

[11] "From" is missing in the MS, but appears in 12,175.

From the Letter to Philemon

57. Against the thought that provokes anger in us over a brother who accepted money or something else that he needed and is not working to repay it:

> If he has wronged you in any way, or owes you anything, charge that to my account (Phlm 18).

From the Letter of James

58. Against the soul that gets angry swiftly but seeks the righteousness of God:

> Let everyone be quick to listen, slow to speak, slow to anger; for your anger does not produce God's righteousness (Jas 1:19-20).

59. Against the thought that has filled the intellect with anger but wants to see its soul in God's wisdom:

> But the wisdom from above is first pure, then peaceable, gentle, willing to yield, full of mercy and good fruits, without a trace of partiality or hypocrisy. And a harvest of righteousness is sown in peace for those who make peace (Jas 3:17-18).

60. Against the thought that is moved by slander of the brothers and scorns the lawgiver—"He did not act justly when he established this law that he commanded, saying, 'Do not slander your brother'":

> Do not speak evil against one another, brothers. Whoever speaks evil against another or judges another, speaks evil against the law and judges the law; but if you judge the law, you are not a doer of the law, but a judge. There is one lawgiver and judge who is able to save and to destroy (Jas 4:11-12).

From the Letter of Peter

61. Against the intellect that wants to repay evil for evil or abuse for abuse and does not want, through blessings, to forget abusive and slanderous thoughts:

> Do not repay evil for evil or abuse for abuse; but, on the contrary, repay with a blessing. It is for this that you were called—so that you might inherit a blessing (1 Pet 3:9).

From the Letter of John

62. Against the intellect that has said that the fear of God is in it but hates its brother:

> Whoever says, "I am in the light," while hating a brother, is still in darkness (1 John 2:9).

63. Against the thoughts that are born of hatred and make the intellect murderous toward a brother:

> All who hate a brother are murderers, and you know that murderers do not have eternal life dwelling in them (1 John 3:15).

64. Against the intellect that professes to love God but, thanks to hatred toward a brother, has renounced the earlier love:

> Those who say, "I love God," and hate their brothers, are liars; for those who do not love a brother whom they have seen, cannot love God whom they have not seen (1 John 4:20).

Blessed is our Lord Jesus Christ, our God, who has given us the victory over the thoughts of the demon of anger, so that we might defeat it!

SIXTH BOOK

Against the Thoughts of the Demon of Listlessness

From Genesis

1. Against the thought of the demon of listlessness that hates the manual labor of the skill that it knows, and wants to learn another skill by which it will be better supported and which will not be so arduous:

   > By the sweat of your face you shall eat bread, until you return to the earth from which you were taken. For you are earth, and to earth you shall return (Gen 3:19).[1]

From Exodus

2. Against the thought that because of listlessness is moved to slander the abbot on the pretext, "He does not comfort the brothers, but he is harsh with them and does not show them mercy in their afflictions":

   > You shall not revile the gods nor speak evilly of the rulers of your people (Exod 22:27).[2]

---

[1] The entries in this book are numbered 330 through 386 in 12,175.
[2] MS and 12,175: "You shall not revile the priest of God . . ."

From Numbers

3. Against the soul that succumbs to the thought of listlessness and impatiently expects to be filled with the fruits of the knowledge of truth:

> You shall persevere and take the fruits of the land (Num 13:21).

From Deuteronomy

4. Against the intellect that because of thoughts of listlessness has inclined itself again to the world and loves it [the world] and the affairs that arise from it:

> Hear, Israel, the Lord our God, the Lord is one. And you shall love the Lord your God with all your mind and with all your soul and with all your strength (Deut 6:4–5).

5. Against the thought of listlessness that deprives us of reading and instruction in spiritual words, leading us astray as it says, "Look, such-and-such holy old man knew only twelve Psalms, and he pleased God":

> And let these words, all that I have commanded you today, be in your heart and in your soul. And you shall teach them to your sons, and you shall speak of them sitting in your house, walking on the road, lying down, and rising up (Deut 6:6–7).

6. Against the soul that receives thoughts of listlessness whenever a little ailment comes upon the body:

> And the Lord will remove from you all sickness, and he will not lay upon you any of the evil diseases of Egypt that you have seen and known, but he will lay them upon those who hate you (Deut 7:15).

7. Against the thought that because of listlessness wants its family and the people of its household and thinks, "The demon of

listlessness is stronger than we are, and I cannot defeat the thoughts that come forth from it and oppose me":

> The Lord your God will hand over your enemies who oppose you utterly broken before you; they will come forth against you on one road, and on seven roads they will flee from before you (Deut 28:7).

From Joshua Son of Nun

8. Against the thought of listlessness that shuns the reading of and meditation on spiritual words and which advises us to ask the Lord that we might learn the Scriptures through his Spirit:

> And the book of this law shall not depart from your mouth, and you shall meditate on it day and night, so that you may know how to do all the things that are written, and you will prosper . . . Look, I have commanded you (Josh 1:8-9).

From Judges

9. Against the soul that at the time of listlessness considers and says, "Why does the Lord so permit me to be tested by the demons? Sometimes they stir up our anger against the brothers who are near us, but at other times they cast us into sadness by compelling us to be annoyed with the brothers who are far from us as well"—these are the tricks of the thoughts of listlessness:

> And the Lord became very angry with Israel and said, "Inasmuch as this nation has abandoned my covenant, which I commanded their fathers, and has not listened to my voice, for my part I will no longer cast out from before them a man from the nations that Joshua the son of Nun left in the land." And he left Israel to be tested by them, [to see] whether they would keep the way of the Lord, to walk in it, as their fathers kept it, or not. So the Lord left these nations so as not to cast them out quickly, and he did not deliver them into the hand

of Joshua. And these are the nations that the Lord left to test Israel by them, all who had not known the wars of Canaan, but on account of the generations of sons of Israel, to teach them warfare, only those who had not before known them (Judg 2:20–3:2).

From David

10. Against the hardened soul that does not want to shed tears at night because of thoughts of listlessness—for the shedding of tears is a great remedy for nocturnal visions that are born from listlessness, and David the prophet wisely applied this remedy to his passions when he said:

> I am wearied with my groaning; I will wash my bed every night; with tears I will water my couch (Ps 6:7).

11. To the Lord concerning the thoughts of listlessness that persist in me:

> Look upon my affliction and my trouble, and forgive all my sins (Ps 24:18).

12. Against the thoughts of listlessness that take away my hope:

> I believe that I will see the good things of the Lord in the land of the living (Ps 26:13).

13. Against the thought of murmuring that derives from listlessness and that dares to be silent concerning praise:

> I will bless the Lord at all times; his praise will be continually in my mouth (Ps 33:2).

14. Against the soul that in listlessness receives thoughts that take away its hope by showing it how very difficult the monastic life is and that a human being can scarcely endure its way of life:

> Hope in the Lord, and do kindness; dwell in the land, and you will be fed with its wealth (Ps 36:3).

15. Against the miserable soul that is listless and chooses other places in which to live:

> Wait on the Lord, and keep his way, and he will raise you up to inherit the land (Ps 36:34).

16. Against the intellect that does not know that, when thoughts of listlessness persist in it, they trouble its stability, and at the time of prayer they obscure the holy light in its eyes—concerning this light, I and God's servant Ammonius wanted to know where it comes from, and we asked the holy John, the seer of Thebes, whether it is the nature of the intellect to be luminous and thus it pours forth the light from itself or whether it [the light] appears from something else outside and illumines it [the intellect]; but he answered us and said, "No human being is able to explain this, and indeed, apart from the grace of God the intellect cannot be illumined in prayer by being set free from the many cruel enemies that are endeavoring to destroy it":

> My heart is troubled; my strength has left me; and the light of my eyes is not with me (Ps 37:11).

17. Against the soul that wants to learn whether the soul truly is handed over to temptations from demons whenever it is briefly abandoned by the holy angels:

> My friends and neighbors drew near before me and stood, and my nearest of kin stood far off, while those who seek my soul pressed hard upon me, and those who seek evil things for me spoke empty things and plotted deceits the entire day (Ps 37:12-13).

18. Against the thought of listlessness that takes away the hope of our endurance on the pretext that one cannot through its duration persuade the Lord to have mercy on us:

> I waited patiently for the Lord, and he attended to me and listened to my supplication (Ps 39:2).

19. Against the soul that supposes that tears are of no benefit at the time of combat with listlessness and that does not remember that David did this very thing, saying to God:

> My tears have been my bread day and night (Ps 41:4).

20. Against the soul that succumbs to listlessness and becomes filled with thoughts of sadness:

> Why are you sad, my soul? And why do you trouble me? Hope in God, for I will give thanks to him, the salvation of my countenance and my God (Ps 41:6).[3]

21. To the Lord concerning the demon of listlessness that contends with me all day:

> Have mercy upon me, Lord, for humanity has tread upon me and afflicted me by making war all day (Ps 55:2).

22. To the Lord because thoughts of anger and desire have departed from me:

> We went through fire and water, and you brought us out into rest (Ps 65:12).

23. To the Lord concerning the thoughts of listlessness that are in us, "So-and-so, one of our brothers or one of our relatives, has attained and joined a rank of honor and authority, and he has become a powerful man":[4]

> It is good for me to cleave to God, to place my hope in the Lord (Ps 72:28).

---

[3] Evagrius elsewhere recommends that the listless monk address this verse to himself: "Whenever we fall in with the demon of listlessness, then we should, with tears, divide our soul in two parts and make one the consoler and the other the object of consolation, sowing good hopes in ourselves and soothing ourselves with David's charm: 'Why are you are sad, my soul, and why do you trouble me? Hope in God, for I will praise him, the salvation of my countenance and my God'" (*Praktikos* 27).

[4] The clause "and he has become a powerful man" does not appear in the MS, but is present in 12,175.

24. Against the thought that entices us at the time of listlessness to journey to the brothers on the pretext of being comforted by them:

> My soul refused to be comforted. I remembered God and rejoiced; I poured out my complaint, and my soul fainted (Ps 76:3-4).

25. Against the thought of listlessness that reckons for me a long time and years of a wretched life:

> As for a human being, his days are like grass; as a flower of the field, so will he flourish (Ps 102:15).

26. Against the thought of listlessness that is eager to find another cell for its dwelling place on the pretext that the first one that it had was very foul and full of moisture so that it got all kinds of diseases from it:

> Here I will dwell, for I have chosen it (Ps 131:14).

27. To the Lord concerning the thoughts that persecute and terrify my intellect:

> For the enemy has pursued my soul; he has brought my life down to the ground; he has made me dwell in dark places, like those who have been dead for ages. And my spirit was grieved in me; my heart was disturbed within me (Ps 142:3-4).

From the Proverbs of Solomon

28. Against the thought of listlessness that rejects manual labor and leans the body in sleep against the wall:

> How long will you lie down, sluggard? When will you wake from sleep? You sleep a little, and you lie down a little, and you nap for a while, and you fold your arms over your breast for a little. Then poverty comes upon you like an evil traveler, and need like a swift courier (Prov 6:9-11).

29. Against the thought that neglects the labors involved in the service of the commandments:

> **Blessed is the person who begins to help, who depends on hope.**[5]

30. Against the thought of listlessness that complains about the brothers on the pretext that there is no love in them and they do not want to console those who are sad and weary:

> **A man who wishes to separate from his friends looks for excuses, but at all times he is liable to reproach** (Prov 18:1).[6]

From Job

31. Against the soul that is saddened because of a thought of listlessness:

> **Do not reject the chastening of the Almighty, for he causes pain, and then he restores again; he smites, and his hands heal. Six times he will deliver you from distresses, and the seventh time evil will not touch you** (Job 5:17-19).

32. Against the thought of listlessness that depicts to us a prolonged old age, severe poverty without consolation, and diseases that can kill the body:

> **Ask the former generation, and search diligently among the race of the fathers; for we are of yesterday and do not understand, for our life upon the earth is a shadow** (Job 8:8-9).

33. Against the thought of listlessness that shows us other places and advises us to acquire a cell there on the pretext that there we will be able to meet our needs without toil and [to provide] peace and consolation to the brothers who come to us:

> **Is not the extent of my life short? Permit me to rest a little before I go where I will not return, to a dark and gloomy land,**

---

[5] The reference is not identified.
[6] For a similar use of Prov 18:1, see *To Monks* 89.

to a land of eternal darkness, where there is no light nor does anyone see the life of mortals (Job 10:20–22).

34. Against the soul that in listlessness thinks that there is no one who sees its afflictions:

> Do not say that a man has no visitation; indeed, he has a visitation from the Lord (Job 34:9).

From Micah

35. Against the thoughts of listlessness that call blessed those who have dealings with the world:

> For all the nations will walk each in its own way, but we will walk in the name of the Lord our God forever and beyond (Mic 4:5).

36. Against the soul that because of a disease of the body receives thoughts of listlessness:

> I will bear the Lord's anger because I have sinned against him, until he rectifies my cause. And he will perform my judgment and bring me out to the light, and I will see his righteousness (Mic 7:9).

From Isaiah

37. Against the soul that has fallen under the weight of listlessness and cries out due to the sloth that results from thoughts of listlessness:

> Look, all those who oppose you will be put to shame and confounded, for they will be as if they were not, and all your opponents will perish (Isa 41:11).

From Jeremiah

38. Against the soul that, due to the thoughts of sloth and listlessness that have persisted in it, has become weak, has been brought low, and has dissipated in the miseries of its soul; whose strength has been consumed by its great fatigue; whose hope has nearly been destroyed by this demon's force; that has become mad and childish with passionate and doleful tears; and that has no relief from anywhere:

> Thus says the Lord, "Let your voice cease from weeping and your eyes from tears, for there is a reward for your labors, and they will return from the land of your enemies, and your children [will have] an abiding home" (Jer 38:16-17).

39. To the Lord concerning the thoughts of listlessness that shake our endurance and provoke us to take a little break and make an extended visit to our home and kinfolk:

> Lord, act on our behalf for your own sake, for our sins are numerous before you, for we have sinned against you. Lord, you are Israel's endurance, and you save in the time of evils (Jer 14:7-8).

From the Lamentations of Jeremiah

40. Against the thoughts that show us the monastic life, that there are many afflictions and great labors in its discipline:

> The Lord is good to those who wait for him. The soul that seeks him is good: it will endure and quietly await the salvation of the Lord (Lam 3:25-26).

41. Against the thought that said that a person can acquire purity and stability apart from the monastic life:

> It is good for a man when he bears a yoke in his youth, sits alone, and is silent, because has taken it upon himself. He will give his cheek to the one who strikes him, and he will be filled with reproaches. For the Lord will not reject forever (Lam 3:27-31).

From Daniel

42. To the Lord concerning the thought of listlessness that has grown strong against me:

> Do not hand us over to the end for the sake of your name, and do not disband your covenant, and do not remove your mercy from us for the sake of Abraham your beloved, and for the sake of Isaac your slave and Israel your son.[7]

From the Gospel of Matthew

43. Against the thought of listlessness that advises us to visit our fleshly father:

> Let the dead bury their own dead; but as for you, go and proclaim the kingdom of God (Luke 9:60; cf. Matt 8:22).[8]

44. Against the soul that has succumbed to listlessness and wants to return to its fleshly relatives:

> Everyone who has left houses or brothers or sisters or father or mother or children or fields, for my name's sake, will receive a hundredfold and will inherit eternal life (Matt 19:29).

From the Gospel of Luke

45. Against the soul that is not convinced that Christ called love toward its family hatred, when he spoke in this way to souls that are in the passions of desires and that love the world:

> Whoever comes to me and does not hate father and mother, wife and children, brothers and sisters, yes, and even life itself, cannot be my disciple (Luke 14:26).

From Acts

46. Against the thoughts of listlessness that are in us on the pretext, "Look, our relatives are saying about us that it is not on

---

[7] Dan 3:34-35 Theod.
[8] See *Foundations of the Monastic Life* 5.

account of God that we have left the world and embraced monasticism, but on account of our sins or on account of our weakness, because we could not excel in the affairs of the world":

We must obey God rather than human beings (Acts 5:29).

From the Letter to the Romans

47. Against the thoughts of listlessness that come upon us due to afflictions:

Be patient in suffering, persevere in prayer (Rom 12:12).

From the First Letter to the Corinthians

48. Against the thoughts that due to listlessness dare to murmur:

Do not complain as some of them did, and were destroyed by the destroyer (1 Cor 10:10).

From the Second Letter to the Corinthians

49. Against the thought that is saddened because of thoughts of listlessness and that does not remember the Apostle's trials, which he recounted, saying:

. . . with far greater labors, far more imprisonments, with countless floggings, and often near death. Five times I have received from the Jews the forty lashes minus one. Three times I was beaten with rods. Once I received a stoning. Three times I was shipwrecked; for a night and a day I was adrift at sea; on frequent journeys, in danger from rivers, danger from bandits, danger from my own people, danger from Gentiles, danger in the city, danger in the wilderness, danger at sea, danger from false brothers; in toil and hardship, through many a sleepless night, hungry and thirsty, often without food, cold and naked. And besides other things . . . (2 Cor 11:23–28).

From <the Letter> to the Ephesians

50. Against the thoughts of listlessness that do not give thanks for the fathers and brothers:

> . . . giving thanks to God the Father at all times and for everything in the name of our Lord Jesus Christ. Be subject to one another out of reverence for Christ (Eph 5:20-21).

From <the Letter> to the Philippians

51. Against the soul that does not know that for a human being to suffer for Christ is a gift given by the Spirit:

> For he has graciously granted you the privilege not only of believing in Christ, but of suffering for him as well—since you are having the same struggle . . . (Phil 1:29-30).

From the Letter to the Hebrews[9]

52. Against the soul's thoughts that have been set in motion by listlessness and want to abandon the holy path of the illustrious ones and its dwelling place:

> For you need endurance, so that when you have done the will of God, you may receive what was promised. For yet "in a very little while the one who is coming will come and will not delay; but my righteous one will live by faith. My soul takes no pleasure in anyone who shrinks back" (Heb 10:36-38).

53. Against the thought that entices us to see the city, my family, and my loved ones there:

> For here we have no lasting city, but we are looking for the city that is to come (Heb 13:14).

54. Against the soul that has succumbed to listlessness and sadness and in its heart reckons that it has been handed over to the punishment of the demons:

> Others suffered mocking and flogging, and even chains and imprisonment. They were stoned to death, they were sawn

---

[9] "The Letter" is missing in the MS, but appears in 12,175.

in two, they were killed by the sword; they went about in skins
of sheep and goats, destitute, persecuted, tormented—of
whom the world was not worthy. They wandered in deserts
and mountains, and in caves and holes in the ground (Heb
11:36-38).

55. Against the thoughts of listlessness that are angry with the
holy fathers on the pretext that they are unfeeling and do
not want to console the brothers, and therefore these thoughts
are fed up with them and do not want to submit to them:

> Obey your leaders and submit to them, for they are keeping
> watch over your souls and will give an account. Let them do
> this with joy and not with sighing (Heb 13:17).

From the Letter of James

56. Against the thought of the soul that is saddened because of
the spirit of listlessness that has persisted in it and altered its
condition:

> My brothers, whenever you face trials of any kind, consider it
> nothing but joy, because you know that the testing of your
> faith produces endurance; and let endurance have its full effect,
> so that you may be mature and complete, lacking in nothing
> (Jas 1:2-4).

57. Against the intellect that due to a thought of listlessness is
thrown all over the place, at one time driven from places by
anger, then at another time dragged by the throat to other
places near the brothers, or to relatives in the world—a condition that has often humiliated and wearied it:

> Blessed is anyone who endures temptation. Such a one has
> stood the test and will receive the crown of life that God has
> promised to those who love him (Jas 1:12).

Blessed is our Lord Jesus Christ, who gives us the victory over
the thoughts of the demon of listlessness!

SEVENTH BOOK

Against the Thoughts from the Demon of Vainglory

From Genesis

1. Against the thought from the demon of vainglory that advises us to go forth into the world at an improper time on the pretext that we might instruct the brothers and sisters and persuade them to [take up] the monastic life:

> Save your own soul. Do not look back or remain in the entire surrounding area. Escape to the mountain, lest perhaps you be overtaken (Gen 19:17).[1]

From Numbers

2. Against the thought of vainglory that stirs up in me jealousy toward the brothers who have received from the Lord the gift of knowledge:

> Are you jealous of me? Would that all the Lord's people were given to be prophets when the Lord gives his Spirit upon them (Num 11:29).

---

[1] The aleph indicating the entry number "1" is written in the margin in the MS, although it does not appear in Frankenberg's text. The entries in this book are numbered 387 through 430 in 12,175, which skips the number 419.

3. Against the soul that has received unclean thoughts, desires the priesthood because of the vainglory that has seized it, and does not recognize the danger that follows it [the priesthood]:

> And Eleazar, the son of Aaron the priest, took the bronze censers, which those who had been burnt brought near, and put them as a covering for the altar, as a reminder to the children of Israel that no foreigner may come near who is not from the seed of Aaron to offer incense before the Lord; and so he shall not be like Korah and those who conspired with him, just as the Lord said by the hand of Moses (Num 17:4–5).[2]

From Deuteronomy

4. Against the thought of vainglory that performs righteousness on account of human beings:

> You shall pursue righteousness justly, so that you may live and go in and inherit the land that the Lord your God gives you (Deut 16:20).[3]

5. Against the thought of vainglory that is yoked with a saying about ascetic achievements and pulls the plough of vainglory:

> You shall not plough with an ox and an ass together (Deut 22:10).

From Samuel

6. Against the thought of vainglory, "Look, you are honored among all the brothers":

> I am a humble person and not honored (1 Kgdms 18:23).

---

[2] On the danger of ordination to the priesthood (7.8, 26, 36, 40), see also *Thoughts* 21, 28.

[3] The daleth indicating the entry number "4" is written in the margin in the MS, although it does not appear in Frankenberg's text.

From the Book of Kings

7. Against the soul that because of vainglory does not want to leave a place that is not suitable for habitation:

> And the sons of the prophets said to Elisha, "Look, the place where we live before you is too constricted for us. Let us go to the Jordan, each man taking there one beam, and let us make for ourselves there a place to live." And he said, "Go" (4 Kgdms 6:1-2).

From David

8. Against the soul that, because of the vainglory that has seized it, supposes that the demons were speaking the truth when they promised it the priesthood:

> For there is no truth in their mouth; their heart is vain; their throat is an open tomb; with their tongues they have deceived (Ps 5:10).

9. Against the thought of vainglory that incites us to teach the brothers and the worldly people when we have not yet acquired health of the soul:

> For the sparrow has found itself a home and the turtledove a nest for herself, where she may lay her young, your altars, Lord of hosts (Ps 83:4).

10. Against the thoughts of vainglory that render the intellect useless with all kinds of thoughts, sometimes making it the steward of God's wealth and sometimes appointing it overseer of the brothers:

> Depart from me, evildoers, and I will investigate my God's commandments (Ps 118:115).

11. Against the thought of vainglory that advises me sternly to withdraw from the brotherhood and to cloister myself from the brothers, supposing that they lead me astray:

> The proud have hidden a snare for me (Ps 139:6).

From the Proverbs of Solomon

12. Against the thought of vainglory that compelled us to talk a lot about superfluous things—this excess becomes quickly apparent in monks who live in seclusion but who, due to vainglory, throw themselves into the affairs of the world and gladly welcome people who come to them to settle disputes they have with one another:

> By talking a lot you will not escape sin, but by using your lips sparingly you will be prudent (Prov 10:19).

13. Against the thought that advised us before we have reached stability to preside over the brothers and lead their souls in the knowledge of Christ:

> There is a way that seems to people to be right, but its ends lead to the depths of Hades (Prov 14:12).

14. Against the thought of vainglory that entices us to give up the Scriptures from then on because we have not grasped their power:

> Whoever answers a word before he has heard, it is a folly and a reproach to him (Prov 18:13).

15. Against the thought of vainglory that encourages those who are very young to settle by themselves:

> Let the one who acts be restrained in his pursuits; let a youth be with a holy person, and his way will be straight (Prov 20:11).[4]

16. Against the thought of vainglory that advised us to give surety for the worldly people who love us when the creditor was harassing them:

> Do not give yourself as surety out of respect for reputation, for if they do not have the means to pay back, they will take the bed out from under you (Prov 22:26-27).

---

[4] MS:"By his actions a youth will be known, if he is devout and his actions are straight."

17. Against the soul that because of vainglory tells some of the secrets of the monastic life to worldly people:

> Speak nothing into a fool's ears, lest he ever sneer at your wise words (Prov 23:9).

18. Against the thoughts that entice us to go out in the world in order to benefit those who see us:

> The words of crafty persons are gentle, but they strike into the depths of the bowels (Prov 26:22).

19. Against the demon that, concerning the great temptations that attack us openly, again persuades us to permit it [to attack]—this, as the holy prophet John told us, it does on account of vainglory; we should answer it as the blessed one answered it, saying:

> A weeping enemy promises everything with his lips, but in his heart he contrives deceit. If the enemy begs you with a loud voice, do not be persuaded, for there are seven abominations is his soul (Prov 26:24–25).

20. Against the thoughts that compel us because of vainglory to make known our illustrious way of life:

> Let your neighbor praise you, and not your own mouth, a stranger and not your own lips (Prov 27:2).

From Qoheleth

21. Against the thought of vainglory that compelled us to speak when we should not and advised us to be silent when we should speak:

> A time to be silent and a time to speak (Qo 3:7).

From Job

22. Against the soul that is not convinced that Satan as well knows those who serve the Lord:

> The devil answered and said before the Lord, "Does Job worship the Lord for nothing? Have you not made a hedge around

him, around his household, and around all that is his? You have
blessed the works of his hands, and you have made his cattle
numerous upon the land" (Job 1:9–10).

From Isaiah

23. Against the demon that advised us, saying, "I will make you
illustrious everywhere before all people," and pretended that
it would help us:

> But the Lord of hosts will send dishonor upon your honor, and
> burning fire will be kindled against your glory (Isa 10:16).

24. Against the soul that loves glory from human beings more
than the knowledge of Christ:

> All flesh is grass, and all the glory of humanity is like the flower
> of grass. The grass withers, and the flower fades, but the word
> of our God endures forever (Isa 40:6–8).[5]

From Jeremiah

25. To the Lord concerning thoughts of glory that persisted in
us and that bring down an intellect that the demons of anger,
sadness, and pride have already wounded:[6]

> Heal me, Lord, and I shall be healed; save me, and I shall be
> saved; for you are my boast (Jer 17:14).

From the Lamentations of Jeremiah

26. Against the demon that, while I was asleep at night, made me
the shepherd of a flock and, during the day, interpreted the

---

[5] See *Exhortation to a Virgin* 18.

[6] The translation of this entry is uncertain; there may be a corruption in the
text. In place of "pride," 12,175 reads "vainglory."

dream for me, saying, "You will be a priest, and look, those who want you will soon come after you":[7]

> They destroyed my life in a pit, and they laid a stone upon me (Lam 3:53).

From Daniel

27. Against the demon that attacked our intellect and said, "Look, soon you will be caught up to heaven" (cf. 2 Cor 12:2)—some of the brothers have thought this and have plunged into a fierce tempest and suffered shipwreck:

> Well have you lied against your own head, for already God's angel has received the sentence from God to cut you in two (Sus 55).

28. Against the demon that promised us in our heart that it would through wisdom make us famous among kings and rulers:

> Well have you lied against your own head, for the angel of God waits, sword in hand, to cut you in two, in order to destroy you (Sus 59).

From the Gospel of Matthew

29. Against the thought of vainglory that, before doing the commandments of God, wants to teach them to the brothers:

> Whoever does them and teaches them will be called great in the kingdom of heaven (Matt 5:19).

30. Against the thought of vainglory that completely attached itself to acts of piety and made the intellect perverse:

> Beware of practicing your piety before others in order to be seen by them; for then you have no reward from your Father in heaven (Matt 6:1).[8]

---

[7] See *Praktikos* 13.

[8] Evagrius cites Matt 6:1, 5, 16, as here and in the following entries, also in *Thoughts* 3 in his discussion of how the Lord can heal the monk of vainglory.

31. Against the thought of vainglory that appears to us in the condition of pure prayer and likens the intellect to the form that it wants, although the intellect is invisible and formless, and depicts it [the intellect] praying to the divine—this happens to the intellect that is troubled by the passion of vainglory and comes from the demon that at the time of prayer approaches its place on the pretext that it might show what is visible to many children and women—let the one who can understand, understand:[9]

> And whenever you pray, do not be like the hypocrites; for they love to stand and pray in the synagogues and in the streets, so that they may be seen by others. Truly I tell you, they have received their reward (Matt 6:5).

32. Against the thoughts of vainglory that endeavor through a sad appearance to reveal our fasting, as if the intellect had been set free and released from thoughts of gluttony, in order that the intellect may be bound and held captive by the thought of vainglory—the filthy demons plot to do this so that the intellect will not be able to stand and fix its gaze on God, transcending thoughts:

> And whenever you fast, do not look dismal, like the hypocrites, for they disfigure their faces so as to show others that they are fasting. Truly I tell you, they have received their reward (Matt 6:16).

33. Against the thoughts of vainglory that compel the soul to speak in empty words, and that endeavor to entangle the intellect in transitory affairs, by which they set in motion in us either desire or anger, or that depict in the intellect obscene visions that spoil the condition of purity that adorns and crowns our prayer:

---

[9] Evagrius taught that the demon of vainglory can manipulate the brain's physiology so as to produce false effects of pure prayer (*Chapters on Prayer* 72).

I tell you, on the day of judgment you will have to give an account for every careless word you utter; for by your words you will be justified, and by your words you will be condemned (Matt 12:36–37).

From the Gospel of Luke

34. Against the thoughts that come with the joy that the unclean spirits have fled from our souls:

Do not rejoice at this, that the spirits submit to you, but rejoice that your names are written in heaven (Luke 10:20).

From the Gospel of John

35. Against the demon that said to me in my heart, "Look, you are proficient with the gift of healing that you have received":

When he lies, he speaks according to his own nature, for he is a liar and the father of lies (John 8:44).

From Acts

36. Against the demon that advised us to acquire the priesthood through money:

May your silver perish with you, because you thought you could obtain God's gift with money! (Acts 8:20).

From the First <Letter> to the Corinthians

37. Against the soul that is troubled by vainglory and desires to learn the wisdom of the Greeks:

For the wisdom of this world is foolishness with God (1 Cor 3:19).

From the Second <Letter> to the Corinthians

38. Against the thought of vainglory that wants to boast in the labor of the stable way of life:

> Let the one who boasts, boast in the Lord. For it is not the one who commends himself that is approved, but the one whom the Lord commends (2 Cor 10:17-18).

From the Letter to the Galatians[10]

39. Against the thought of vainglory that encourages us to persuade our relatives that if we live justly in the monastic life we will be worthy of the soul's health and knowledge of the truth:

> Am I now seeking human approval, or God's approval? Or am I trying to please people? If I were still pleasing people, I would not be a slave of Christ (Gal 1:10).

From the Letter to the Hebrews[11]

40. Against the thought of vainglory that advises me to do something so that I might be honored with the priesthood:

> And one does not presume to take this honor, but takes it only when called by God (Heb 5:4).

From the Letter of James

<41.> Against the thought of vainglory that encourages us to teach although we have not acquired the soul's health or knowledge of the truth:

> Not many of you should become teachers, my brothers, for you know that we who teach will be judged with greater

---

[10] "The Letter" is missing in the MS, but appears in 12,175.
[11] "The Letter" is missing in the MS, but appears in 12,175.

strictness. For all of us make many mistakes. Anyone who makes no mistakes in speaking is perfect, able to keep the whole body in check with a bridle (Jas 3:1–2).

42. Against the thoughts of vainglory that request gifts of healing or knowledge of God:

> You ask and do not receive, because you ask wrongly, in order to spend what you get on your pleasures [Jas 4:3].

From the Letter of John

43. Against the thoughts of vainglory that seek the world and depict its glory before our eyes:

> Do not love the world or the things in the world. The love of the Father is not in those who love the world (1 John 2:15).

Blessed is our Lord Jesus Christ, who has given us the victory over the thoughts of the demon of vainglory!

EIGHTH BOOK

Against the Cursed Thoughts of Pride

From the Book of Genesis

1. Against the thought of pride that said to me, "I am the Lord's holy one":

   > You are cursed above all cattle and all the beasts upon the earth. You will go on your breast and on your belly, and you will eat dirt all the days of your life (Gen 3:14).[1]

2. Against the thought of pride that glorifies me and exalts me on the pretext that I am pure and no longer receive filthy thoughts:

   > Now I have begun to speak to my Lord, but I am earth and ashes (Gen 18:27).[2]

3. Against the blasphemous thought that denied that God feeds me and that rejects the angel that assists me:

   > God, who continues to feed me from my youth until this day; the angel, who rescues me from all evils (Gen 48:15–16).

---

[1] The entries in this book are numbered 431 through 495 in 12,175, which actually has 496 entries. See the Note on Texts and Translations for discussion of the numbering system in 12,175.

[2] As an antidote to pride Evagrius recommends that the monk remind himself that he is earth and ashes (*Eight Thoughts* 8.12; *Exhortations* 1.6).

From Exodus

4. Against the soul that wants to learn what the proud demons say when they see us investigating spiritual matters:

> **Let the tasks of these people be burdensome, and let them care about these things and not care about empty words** (Exod 5:9).

5. Against the proud thought that rejected the salvation of God, by whose help we defeat the seven other demons, the companions of the demon of pride:

> **Let us sing to the Lord, for he is greatly glorified: horse and rider he has thrown into the sea. He was to me a helper and protector for salvation** (Exod 15:1-2).

6. To the Lord concerning the thought of pride that glorifies me on the pretext that by my great strength I have cast down the demons of sadness:

> **Your right hand, Lord, has been glorified in strength; your right hand, Lord, has broken the enemies. And in the abundance of your glory you have broken the adversaries to pieces** (Exod 15:6-7).

7. Against the thoughts of pride that compel the soul to scorn the holy angels on the pretext that they cannot instruct it about the mistakes that it makes, so that it abandons them because it thinks these things and it succumbs again to the filthy demons, that is, the thoughts of pride:

> **Look, I am sending my angel before you, so that he may keep you on the way and lead you into the land that I have prepared for you. Pay attention to him and listen to him, and do not disobey him, for he will not give way to you, for my name is upon him** (Exod 23:20-21).

From the Book of Leviticus

8. Against the thought of pride that advised us to scorn our holy fathers on the pretext that they have not labored in their way of life any more than we have:

> You shall rise before a venerable face, and you shall honor the face of an elder, and you shall fear your God (Lev 19:32).

9. Against the blasphemous thought that sends the intellect into utter ruin:

> Whichever human being curses God shall bear his sin. Whoever names the name of the Lord, let him perish utterly; let the entire congregation of Israel stone him with stones (Lev 24:15–16).

\<From Numbers\>

10. To the Lord because blasphemous thoughts persist in us and destroy the frankness of prayer:

> Arise, Lord, and let your enemies be scattered; let all that hate you flee (Num 10:35).[3]

11. Against the soul that does not know the beauty of knowledge and is convinced by the demon that has advised it to shun the knowledge of Christ and the holy commandments, which it [the demon] belittles before our eyes:

> But from among those who spied out the land, Joshua son of Nun and Caleb son of Jephunneh tore their garments and said to the entire congregation of the sons of Israel, "The land that we surveyed is very good. If the Lord chose us, he will lead us into this land and give it to us, a land flowing with milk and honey. Only do not depart from the Lord" (Num 14:6–9).

From Deuteronomy

12. Against the blasphemous thought that made us consider whether God is in us or not:

> You shall not tempt the Lord your God (Deut 6:16).

---

[3] The yod representing the entry number "10" is present in the MS, although it does not appear in Frankenberg's text.

13. Against the soul that proudly supposes that by its own strength it has conquered the demons that oppose our doing the commandments:

> Do not say in your heart, "My strength and the might of my hand have made for me this great power." But you shall remember the Lord your God, who gives you the strength (Deut 8:17–18).

14. Against the intellect that has supposed that because of its righteousness and justice it has defeated its enemies and has entered and inherited the knowledge of Christ:

> When the Lord your God has destroyed these enemies from before you, do not say in your heart, "Because of my righteousness the Lord has brought me in to inherit this good land." Not because of your righteousness and not because of your heart's holiness do you go in to inherit their land; rather, because of the wickedness of these nations, the Lord will destroy them from before you (Deut 9:4–5).

15. Against the demon that said to me that all people bless me and that I am the progenitor of sages:

> You are cursed in the city, and you are cursed in the field. Cursed are your barns and your storehouses. Cursed are the offspring of your belly and the fruits of your land (Deut 28:16–17).[4]

16. Against the blasphemous thought that denied the free will that is in us and said that we sin and are justified not by our own will and therefore condemnation is not decreed justly:

> Look, I have set before you this day life and death, good and evil (Deut 30:15).

---

[4] The manuscript numbers both this saying and the following one 16.

From Joshua the Son of Nun

17. Against the thoughts of the soul that is not aware that it should not suppose that every angel that suddenly appears to it belongs to the Lord, rather only if, when it speaks, it gives joy and perfect peace to the soul, after its appearance had brought trembling and fear—but the demons in their appearance do not impart this peace; rather, they cast great fear and trembling into the soul and body, and through their hollow voice they bring agitation and disorder upon the heart:[5]

> And it happened that when Joshua was in Jericho, he looked up and saw with his eyes a person standing in front of him with a drawn sword in his hand. And Joshua approached him and said, "Do you belong to us or our enemies?" And he said to him, "It is I, the general of the Lord's hosts, who has now come." And Joshua fell on his face on the earth and said to him, "Lord, what do you command your servant?" (Josh 5:13-14).

From Samuel

18. Against the thought of pride that denied God's grace:

> If a man should sin greatly against a man, still they will pray for him to the Lord. But if he sins against the Lord, who will pray for him? (1 Kgdms 2:25).

From the Book of Kings

19. Against the soul that wants and is pleased to kneel, and works to humiliate the blasphemous demon that stops our ceaseless prayers:

> And Elijah went up to Carmel and stooped to the ground and put his face between his knees (3 Kgdms 18:42).

[5] This teaching may be compared to *Life of Antony* 43.

20. Against the soul that is shaken by the frightening thoughts of blasphemy and falls away from the frankness[6] of prayer:

> Do not be afraid of the words that you have heard, by which the Assyrian king's slaves have blasphemed. Look, I am putting a spirit in him, and he will hear a report, and he will return to his own land, and I will overthrow him with the sword in his own land (4 Kgdms 19:6-7).

21. To the Lord concerning the words by which the demon spoke in us unspeakable blasphemies against the Lord, things that I cannot write, lest I shake heaven and earth; for in anger this demon stands without fear and speaks great blasphemy against God and the holy angels—those who have been tempted by it understand what I am saying—and at the time of this temptation what is excellent is fasting, reading of the Scriptures, and unceasing[7] prayers offered with tears:

> Lord God of Israel, who dwells over the cherubim, you are the only God in all the kingdoms of the earth; you made heaven and earth. Incline your ear, Lord, and hear; open your eyes, Lord, and see; and hear the words of Semmacherim, which he has sent to reproach the living God (4 Kgdms 19:15-16).

From Ezra

<22.> To the Lord concerning the thought of pride that denied that the victory comes from God:

> From you comes victory, and from you comes wisdom, and yours is the glory, and I am your servant. Blessed are you, who gave me wisdom, and I confess you, ruler of our fathers (1 Esd 4:59-60).

---

[6] Frankenberg's text reads "power" (*ḥyl*ʾ), which is the original reading in the MS. But an ancient corrector marked this word and wrote in the margin "frankness" (*prʾsyʾ*), which is the original reading in 12,175.

[7] Frankenberg's text reads *dlʾ qtʿn*, but in the MS an ancient corrector has marked this word and written in the margin *ʾmyntʾ*, which is the original reading in 12,175. The meaning is the same in either case.

From David

23. To the Lord concerning blasphemous thoughts that have persisted in me:

> Lord my God, in you I have hoped: save me from all those who persecute me, and rescue me, lest he ever seize my soul like a lion, without anyone to ransom or to save (Ps 7:2-3).

24. To the Lord concerning the demon of pride that has approached us and that often appears like an angel of light (cf. 2 Cor 11:14), leading a great army of demons with it:

> Let not the foot of pride come against me, and let not the hand of sinners shake me (Ps 35:12).[8]

25. To the Lord concerning the thought of pride that denied God's help and attributed victory to its own strength:

> For I will not hope in my bow, and my sword will not save me. For you saved us from those who afflict us, and you have put to shame those who hate us (Ps 43:7-8).

26. Against the demon that promises to interpret the Scriptures for us—we should say as our holy father Macarius said:[9]

> To the sinner God has said, "Why do you declare my ordinances and take my covenant with your mouth? You hated my instruction and cast my words behind you" (Ps 49:16-17).

27. Against the proud thoughts that surround the intellect and cast it into great ruin:

> How long will you besiege a human being? You are all slaughtering by means of a bent wall and a broken fence (Ps 61:4).

---

[8] See *Eight Thoughts* 8.13.

[9] MS: "our father the blessed Macarius"; 12,175: "our father Macarius"; see Guillaumont, "Le problème des deux Macaire," 52.

28. To the Lord concerning proud thoughts that have persisted in us and have caused the intellect to lack frankness at the time of prayer:

> **The words of lawless persons have overpowered me, but as for you, pardon our sins** (Ps 64:4).

29. Against the thoughts of blasphemy that said unspeakable things concerning the Lord:

> **Do not lift high your horn, and do not speak unrighteousness against God** (Ps 74:6).

30. Against the thought of pride that glorifies me on the pretext that I edify souls with a stable way of life and knowledge of God:

> **Unless the Lord builds the house, the builders labor in vain; unless the Lord guards the city, the guards keep watch in vain** (Ps 126:1).[10]

From the Proverbs of Solomon

31. Against the proud thought that derides the brothers on the pretext, "Look, they are neglecting the service of the commandments":

> **The Lord opposes the proud, but gives grace to the humble** (Prov 3:34).

32. Against the soul that wants to learn what the cruel demons' food is:

> **For they live on the bread of impiety and get drunk on the wine of transgression** (Prov 4:17).

33. Against the proud thought that has prevented me from seeing the brothers on the pretext that they are no better than I am in knowledge:

---

[10] Evagrius says that Ps 126:1 instills humility in the monk (*Praktikos* Prol.2; *Exhortations* 1.6).

> A person who travels with the wise will be wise, but the one who travels with fools will be recognized (Prov 13:20).

34. Against the proud thought that at a time of severe and prolonged temptation prevents me from entreating the Lord through the brothers:

> A brother who is helped by a brother is like a strong and high city (Prov 18:19).

35. Against the proud thought that considered me pure and victorious:

> Who will boast that he has a pure heart? Or who will boldly say that he is pure from sins? (Prov 20:9).

36. Against the proud thought that called success fear:

> Blessed is the man who cowers before all things because of piety, but the hard-hearted one will fall into evils (Prov 28:14).

From Qoheleth

37. Against the proud thoughts that are puffed up against the brothers because of our fleshly birth and suppose that it is glorious:

> Everything goes to one place: everything came from the dust, and everything will return to the dust (Qo 3:20).

38. Against the proud thought that shows me the brothers' sins:

> For there is not a righteous person on earth who will do good and not sin (Qo 7:20).

39. Against the demon that said to me, "Look, you have become a perfect monk":

> There is hope because a living dog is better than a dead lion (Qo 9:4).

From Job

40. Against the demons that "heal" the mature person of humility [and bring him] to the pride of the sick:

> **But you are all unjust physicians and healers of diseases** (Job 13:4).

41. Against the thoughts[11] that seize the intellect into blasphemy against God:

> **Do you not speak before the Lord and utter deceit before him?** (Job 13:7).

42. Against the proud thought that recounted for me the brothers' sins:

> **For who will be pure from uncleanness? Not even one, even if his life were one day upon the earth and he can count its months** (Job 14:4-5).

43. Against the soul that, due to the pride that has seized it, supposes that its way of life is like an acceptable offering before God:

> **For what does it concern the Lord if you were blameless in your works?** (Job 22:3).

From Zechariah

44. Against the thought of the demon that compelled the intellect to commit impiety in heaven:

> **The Lord rebuke you, devil, and the Lord rebuke you, he who has chosen Jerusalem** (Zech 3:2).

From Isaiah

45. Against the proud thought that exalts me as if I were a wise man:

---

[11] Frankenberg's text reads "demons" (*dwyʾ*), but in the MS an ancient corrector marked this word and wrote in the margin "thoughts" (*ḥwšbʾ*), which is the original reading in 12,175.

> Woe to those who are wise in their own eyes and knowing in their own estimation (Isa 5:21).

46. Against the soul that is not convinced that nothing alarms the demons and casts them into fear except the knowledge of Christ, which unmasks all their strategies and uncovers the cruelty of their secret thoughts:

> And the land of the Jews will serve as a terror to the Egyptians: whoever will name it to them they will fear because of the counsel that the Lord of hosts has desired concerning it (Isa 19:17).

From Jeremiah

47. Against the proud and blasphemous thoughts that make the demons gods:

> So speak to them: "Let the gods that did not make heaven and earth perish from the earth and from under this heaven" (Jer 10:11).

48. To the Lord concerning the thought of pride that glorifies me and has said, "Look, you have been victorious over your enemies":

> I know, Lord, that the way of the human being is not his own: a man will not go and direct his own travel (Jer 10:23).

From the Lamentations of Jeremiah

[49a.] Against the soul that is saddened by a blasphemous thought:

> For the Lord will not reject forever. For he that brought down will have pity, even according to the abundance of his mercy. He has not answered from his heart, and he has brought low the sons of a man (Lam 3:31–33).[12]

---

[12] This entry is simply "49" in the MS.

[49b.] To the Lord concerning the blasphemous thoughts that cover the intellect at the time of prayer:

> You have visited in wrath and have driven us away. You have killed and have not shown pity. You have veiled yourself with a cloud because of prayer, so that I will be blind and cast off. You have placed us among the nations (Lam 3:43–45).[13]

From Ezekiel

[49c.] Against the proud demon that names itself God:

> Will you actually say, "It is I who am God," before those who kill you? But you are a human being and not God. You will perish at the hands of foreigners among the multitude of the uncircumcised, for I have spoken, says the Lord (Ezek 28:9–10).

From the Gospel of Matthew[14]

[49d.] Against the soul that despises a brother on the pretext that he is negligent and not diligent and, because it is bound by the fetters of pride, does not recognize the magnitude of this sin:

> Why do you see the speck in your brother's eye, but do not notice the log in your own eye? (Matt 7:3).

[49e.] Against the blasphemous demon that has spoken lies—the unclean foods are thoughts:

> It is not what goes into the mouth that defiles a person, but it is what comes out of the mouth that defiles (Matt 15:11).[15]

---

[13] This entry and the four that follow are not numbered in the MS.

[14] "From" is missing in the MS, but appears in 12,175.

[15] Evagrius could also interpret Matt 15:11 as referring literally to foods (*Foundations of the Monastic Life* 10).

From the Gospel of Mark

[49f.] Against the soul that is oppressed by thoughts of pride and does not know how to drive them out from it:

> This kind can come out only through prayer and fasting (Mark 9:29).

50. For the proud intellect that desires to be first among the brothers:

> Whoever wants to be first must be last of all and servant of all (Mark 9:35).

From the Gospel of Luke

51. Against the proud thought that supposed that it need do nothing more than God's commandments:

> We are worthless slaves; we have only done what we ought to have done (Luke 17:10).[16]

52. Against the proud thought that justifies itself and is not pleased by what is accomplished by the brothers in weakness:

> For all who exalt themselves will be humbled, and those who humble themselves will be exalted (Luke 14:11).

From the Letter to the Romans

53. Against the proud thought that despises a brother who does not eat and considers him to be weak on the pretext, "He is not able to stand in the battle when eating, and therefore he has given himself to fasting":

> Those who eat must not despise those who abstain (Rom 14:3a).

---

[16] See *Foundations of the Monastic Life* 20.

54. Against the proud thought that passed judgment on the one who eats on the pretext, "It is because he cannot control himself":

> And those who abstain must not pass judgment on those who eat (Rom 14:3b).

From the First <Letter> to the Corinthians

55. Against the proud thought that glorifies me on the pretext, "I am able[17] not only not to be enslaved to the belly, but also to conquer anger":

> It was not I, but the grace of God that is with me (1 Cor 15:10).

From the Second <Letter> to the Corinthians

56. Against the soul that is not convinced that even Satan himself imitates an angel of truth and becomes a teacher of false knowledge:

> Even Satan disguises himself as an angel of light. So it is not strange if his ministers also disguise themselves as ministers of righteousness. Their end will match their deeds (2 Cor 11:14–15).

From the Letter to the Galatians[18]

57. Against the proud thoughts that despise the brothers who stumble because of their faults:

> My brothers, if anyone is detected in a transgression, you who have received the Spirit should restore him in a spirit of gentleness. Take care that you yourselves are not tempted (Gal 6:1).

---

[17] The translation "I am able" reads *mṣ'* instead of *mṣl'* (the reading of both the MS and 12,175).

[18] "Letter" is missing in the MS, but appears in 12,175.

From the Letter to the Philippians[19]

58. Against the proud thought that exalts me on the pretext that I have attained perfection in the service of the commandments:

> Not that I have already attained this or have already been made perfect; but I press on to make it my own, because Christ Jesus has made me his own (Phil 3:12).

From the Letter of John

59. Against the proud thought that exalts me on the pretext that there is no image of sin in my thinking:

> If we say that we have no sin, we deceive ourselves, and the truth is not in us. If we confess our sins, he who is faithful and just will forgive our sins and cleanse us from all unrighteousness (1 John 1:8-9).

From the Letter of Jude[20]

60. Against the soul's thoughts that request from the Lord the soul's health until the end:

> Now to him who is able to keep you from falling, and to make you stand without blemish in the presence of his glory with rejoicing, to the only God our Savior, through Jesus Christ our Lord, be glory, majesty, power, and authority, before all time and now and forever. Amen (Jude 24–25).

Blessed is our Lord Jesus Christ, our God, who has given us the victory over the thoughts of the demon of pride!

The end of this book of the blessed Evagrius concerning these eight thoughts and the answering from the Holy Scriptures when the demons tempt us, there being 497 chapters.[21]

---

[19] "Letter" is missing in the MS, but appears in 12,175.

[20] The MS reads: "From the Letter of the Jews." 12,175 has the correct heading.

[21] There are actually 498 entries in the MS. 12,175 reads: "These completed the eight thoughts."

Bibliography

Text of Talking Back

Frankenberg, Wilhelm. *Euagrios Ponticus.* Abhandlungen der königlichen Gesellschaft der Wissenschaften zu Göttingen, Philologisch-historische Klasse, Neue Folge 13.2. Berlin: Weidmannsche Buchhandlung, 1912, 472–544.

Sargisean, Barshegh. *The Life and Works of the Holy Father Evagrius Ponticus in an Armenian Version of the Fifth Century with Introduction and Notes* (in Armenian). Venice: S. Ghazar, 1907, 217–323.

Sims-Williams, Nicholas. *The Christian Sogdian Manuscript C2.* Schriften zur Geschichte und Kultur des alten Orients: Berliner Turfautexte 12. Berlin: Akademie, 1985, 168–82.

Modern Translations of Talking Back

Prologue:
Bunge, Gabriel. "Evagrios Pontikos: Der Prolog des 'Antirretikos.'" *Studia Monastica* 39 (1997): 77–105.

Prologue and Selections from Books 3, 4, and 5:
O'Laughlin, Michael. "Evagrius Ponticus: *Antirrheticus* (Selections)." In *Ascetic Behavior in Greco-Roman Antiquity: A Sourcebook*, edited by Vincent L. Wimbush, 243–62. Studies in Antiquity and Christianity. Minneapolis: Fortress, 1990.

Book 5:
Stewart, Columba. "Evagrius Ponticus on Prayer and Anger." In *Religions of Late Antiquity in Practice*, edited by Richard Valantasis, 65–81. Princeton Readings in Religion. Princeton: Princeton University Press, 2000.

Book 6:
Joest, Christoph. "The Significance of *Acedia* and *Apatheia* in Evagrius Ponticus." Translated by Mark DelCogliano. *American Benedictine Review* 55 (2004): 121–50, 273–307. German original: "Die Bedeutung von Akedia und Apatheia bei Evagrios Pontikos." *Studia Monastica* 35 (1993): 7–53.

Text and Translation of Loukios' Letter to Evagrius

Hausherr, Irénée. "Eulogius—Loukios." *Orientalia Christiana Periodica* 6 (1940): 216–20.

Text and Translation of Evagrius, "Letter 4"

Bunge, Gabriel. *Evagrios Pontikos: Briefe aus der Wüste*. Sophia: Quellen östlicher Theologie 24. Trier: Paulinus, 1986, 214–16.

Frankenberg, Wilhelm. *Euagrios Ponticus*. Abhandlungen der königlichen Gesellschaft der Wissenschaften zu Göttingen, Philologisch-historische Klasse, Neue Folge 13.2. Berlin: Weidmannsche Buchhandlung, 1912, 568.

Guillaumont, Claire. "Fragments grecs inédits d'Evagre le Pontique." In *Texte und Textkritik: Eine Aufsatzsammlung*. Texte und Untersuchungen zur Geschichte der altchristlichen Literatur 133, edited by Jürgen Dummer, 209–21. Berlin: Akademie, 1987.

Other Works of Evagrius

Chapters on Prayer. Text: *Patrologica Graeca* 79:1165–1200. Translation: Evagrius of Pontus. *The Greek Ascetic Corpus*, edited and translated by Robert E. Sinkewicz. Oxford Early Christian Studies. Oxford: Oxford University Press, 2003, 183–209.

Letters. Text: Frankenberg, *Euagrios Ponticus*, 564–610. Translation: Bunge, Gabriel. *Evagrios Pontikos: Briefe aus der Wüste*. Sophia: Quellen östlicher Theologie 24. Trier: Paulinus, 1986.

Reflections. Text: Muyldermans, J. *Evagriana, Extrait de la revue Le Muséon 44, augmenté de: Nouveaux fragments grecs inédits*. Paris: Paul Geuthner, 1931, 369–83. Translation: Evagrius, *The Greek Ascetic Corpus*, edited and translated by Robert E. Sinkewicz, 210–16.

Thoughts. Text: *Sur les pensées*. Paul Géhin, Claire Guillaumont, and Antoine Guillaumont, eds. Sources chrétiennes 438. Paris: Éditions du Cerf, 1998. Translation: Evagrius, *The Greek Ascetic Corpus*, edited and translated by Robert E. Sinkewicz, 136–82.

Select Additional Ancient Works

Apophthegmata Patrum. Guy, Jean-Claude, ed. *Les apophtegmes des pères: collection systématique*. 3 vols. Sources chrétiennes 387, 474, 498. Paris: Éditions du Cerf, 1993, 2003, 2005.

Athanasius of Alexandria. *Epistle to Marcellinus*. Text: *Patrologia Graeca* 27:11–46. Translation: *The Life of Antony and the Letter to Marcellinus*, translated by Robert C. Gregg, 101–29. Classics of Western Spirituality. New York: Paulist Press, 1980.

———. *The Life of Antony*. Text: *Vie de Antoine*. G. J. M. Bartelink, ed. Sources chrétiennes 400. Paris: Éditions du Cerf, 1994. Translation: *The Life of Antony*. Edited and translated by Tim Vivian and Apostolos N. Athanassakis. Cistercian Studies 202. Kalamazoo: Cistercian Publications, 2003.

Cyprian, *Ad Quirinum, Ad Fortunatum*, ed. R. Weber, Corpus Christionorum Series Latina 3/1 (CCSL 3/1). Turnhout: Brepols, 1972; Cyprian, Treatise 11 [To Fortunatus] and Treatise 12 [to Quirinus], Alexander Roberts and James Donovan, eds., The Ante-Nicene Fathers vols. 5 (ANF 5). New York: Scribner's, 1911, 496–507, 507–557.

Meyer, Marvin, and Richard Smith, eds. *Ancient Christian Magic: Coptic Texts of Ritual Power*. San Francisco: HarperSanFrancisco, 1994.

Palladius. *The Lausiac History*. Text: Butler, Cuthbert. *The Lausiac History of Palladius*. Texts and Studies: Contributions to Biblical and Patristic

Literature 6. 2 vols. Cambridge: Cambridge University Press, 1898–1904. Translation: *The Lausiac History*. Translated by Robert T. Meyer. Ancient Christian Writers 34. New York: Paulist Press, 1964.

————. *Life of Evagrius*. Text: Amélineau, É. *De Historia Lausiaca, quaenam sit huius ad monachorum aegyptorum historiam scribendam utilitas*. Paris: Leroux, 1887, 92–104. Translation: Vivian, Tim. *Four Desert Fathers: Pambo, Evagrius, Macarius of Egypt & Macarius of Alexandria: Coptic Texts Relating to the 'Lausiac History' of Palladius*. Popular Patristics Series. Crestwood, NY: St. Vladimir's Seminary Press, 2004, 69–92.

Plutarch, *De tranquillitate animi*, in Plutarch, *Moralia*, 13 vols., vol. 6, ed. Jeffrey Henderson, The Loeb Classic Library 337. Cambridge: Harvard University, 1939.

Studies

Albl, Martin C. *'And Scripture Cannot Be Broken': The Form and Function of the Early Christian 'Testimonia' Collections*. Supplements to Novum Testamentum 96. Leiden: Brill, 1999.

Augst, Rüdiger. *Lebensverwirklichung und christlicher Glaube Acedia—Religiöse Gleichgültigkeit als Problem der Spiritualität bei Evagrius Ponticus*. Saarbrücker Theologische Forschungen 3. Frankfurt: Peter Lang, 1990.

Brakke, David. "Care for the Poor, Fear of Poverty, and Love of Money: Evagrius Ponticus on the Monk's Economic Vulnerability." In *Wealth and Poverty in Early Church and Society*, edited by Susan Holman, 76–87. Holy Cross Studies in Patristic Theology and History. Grand Rapids, MI: Baker Academic, 2008.

————. *Demons and the Making of the Monk: Spiritual Combat in Early Christianity*. Cambridge, MA: Harvard University Press, 2006.

————. "Making Public the Monastic Life: Reading the Self in Evagrius Ponticus' *Talking Back*." In *Religion and the Self in Antiquity*, edited by David Brakke, Michael L. Satlow, and Steven Weitzman, 222–33. Bloomington: Indiana University Press, 2005.

Bunge, Gabriel. "Évagre le Pontique et les deux Macaire." *Irénikon* 56 (1983): 215–27, 323–60.

―――. "Evagrios Pontikos: Der Prolog des 'Antirretikos.'" *Studia Monastica* 39 (1997): 77–105.

―――. *Akedia: La doctrine spirituelle d'Évagre le Pontique sur l'acédie.* Bégrolles-en-Mauges: Abbaye de Bellefontaine, 1991.

Bunge, Gabriel, and Adalbert de Vogüé. *Quatre ermites égyptiens: d'après les fragments coptes de l' 'Histoire Lausiaque.'* Spiritualité Orientale 60. Bégrolles-en-Mauges: Abbaye de Bellefontaine, 1994.

Clark, Elizabeth A. *The Origenist Controversy: The Cultural Construction of an Early Christian Debate.* Princeton: Princeton University Press, 1992.

―――. *Reading Renunciation: Asceticism and Scripture in Early Christianity.* Princeton: Princeton University Press, 1999.

Dysinger, Luke. *Psalmody and Prayer in the Writings of Evagrius Ponticus.* Oxford Theological Monographs. Oxford: Oxford University Press, 2005.

Foucault, Michel. "Self Writing." In *Ethics: Subjectivity and Truth.* The Essential Works of Michel Foucault, 1954–1984, edited by Paul Rabinow, 207–22. New York: The New Press, 1994.

Gleason, Maud. "Visiting and News: Gossip and Reputation-Management in the Desert." *Journal of Early Christian Studies* 6 (1998): 501–21.

Graver, Margaret R. *Stoicism and Emotion.* Chicago and London: University of Chicago Press, 2007.

Guillaumont, Antoine, and Claire Guillaumont. "Démon: III. Dans la plus ancienne literature monastique." *Dictionnaire de spiritualité ascétique et mystique: Doctrine et histoire* (1957) 3:189–212.

Joest, Christoph. "The Significance of *Acedia* and *Apatheia* in Evagrius Ponticus." Mark DelCogliano, trans. *American Benedictine Review* 55 (2004): 121–50, 273–307. German original: "Die Bedeutung von Akedia und Apatheia bei Evagrios Pontikos." *Studia Monastica* 35 (1993): 7–53.

Kalleres, Dayna. "Demons and Divine Illumination: A Consideration of Certain Prayers by Gregory of Nazianzus." *Vigiliae Christianae* 67 (2007): 157–88.

————. "Exorcising the Devil to Silence Christ's Enemies: Ritualized Speech Practices in Late Antique Christianity." PHD dissertation, Brown University, 2002.

Kelly, Henry Ansgar. *The Devil at Baptism: Ritual, Theology, and Drama* (Ithaca, NY: Cornell University Press, 1985).

Kolbet, Paul R. "Athanasius, the Psalms, and the Reformation of the Self." *Harvard Theological Review* 99 (2006): 85–101.

Layton, Richard A. *Didymus the Blind and his Circle in Late-Antique Alexandria: Virtue and Narrative in Biblical Scholarship.* Urbana, IL: University of Illinois Press, 2004.

————. "Propatheia: Origen and Didymus on the Origin of the Passions." *Vigiliae Christianae* 54 (2000): 262–82.

O'Laughlin, Michael. "The Bible, the Demons, and the Desert: Evaluating the Antirrheticus of Evagrius Ponticus." *Studia Monastica* 34 (1992): 201–15.

Rich, Antony D. *Discernment in the Desert Fathers: 'Diakrisis' in the Life and Thought of Early Egyptian Monasticism.* Studies in Christian History and Thought. Milton Keyes, U.K.: Paternoster, 2007.

Sorabji, Richard. *Emotion and Peace of Mind: From Stoic Agitation to Christian Temptation.* Oxford: Oxford University Press, 2000.

Stewart, Columba. "Imageless Prayer and the Theological Vision of Evagrius Ponticus." *Journal of Early Christian Studies* 9 (2001): 173–204.

Young, Robin Darling. "Cannibalism and Other Family Woes in Letter 55 of Evagrius of Pontus." In *The World of Early Egyptian Christianity: Language, Literature, and Social Context,* edited by James E. Goehring and Janet A. Timbie, 130–39. Washington: The Catholic University of America Press, 2007.

Index of Scripture Passages
Used as Responses

New Testament

Colossians

3:5-6	3.51
3:8-9	5.52

1 Thessalonians

4:10-12	1.63
5:15	5.53

2 Thessalonians

3:10	1.64

1 Timothy

1:5	5.54
5:22-23	1.67
6:7-8	3.53
6:10	3.54

2 Timothy

2:4-5	3.55
2:24	5.55
3:12	5.56

Philemon

18	5.57

Hebrews

5:4	7.40
10:36-38	6.52
11:36-38	6.54
12:11	1.65
13:5	3.52
13:14	6.53
13:16	1.66
13:17	6.55

James

1:2-4	6.56

1:12	6.57
1:13-14	2.61
1:19-20	5.58
3:1-2	7.41
3:17-18	5.59
4:1	2.62
4:3	7.42
4:4	1.68
4:7	4.75
4:11-12	5.60

1 Peter

3:9	5.61
3:13-15	4.76
4:11	3.56
4:12-13	2.63
5:8-9	2.64

2 Peter

2:9	2.65

1 John

1:8-9	8.59
2:9	5.62
2:15	7.43
3:15	5.63
3:17	3.57
3:18	3.58
4:20	5.64
5:3-4	1.69

Jude

24-25	8.60

Unidentified Passages

1.31 (Proverbs or Sirach?)

6.29 (Proverbs?)

Index of Scripture Passages
Excluding Those Used
as Responses